THE BEGINNER'S GUIDE TO GETTING PUBLISHED

6th edition

Chriss McCallum

howtobooks

Published by How To Books Ltd
Spring Hill House, Spring Hill Road,
Begbroke, Oxford OX5 1RX, United Kingdom.
Tel: (01865) 375794. Fax: (01865) 379162.
email: info@howtobooks.co.uk
www.howtobooks.co.uk

How To Books greatly reduce the carbon footprint of their books by sourcing their typesetting and printing in the UK.

Fifth edition 2003
Reprinted 2004
Sixth edition 2008

British Library Cataloguing in Publication Data
A catalogue record for this book is available from the British Library

ISBN 978 1 84528 217 2

Produced for How To Books by Deer Park Productions, Tavistock
Typeset by PDQ Typesetting, Newcastle-under-Lyme, Staffs.
Printed and bound in Great Britain by Bell & Bain Ltd, Glasgow

NOTE: The material contained in this book is set out in good faith for general guidance and no liability can be accepted for loss or expense incurred as a result of relying in particular circumstances on statements made in the book. Laws and regulations are complex and liable to change, and readers should check the current position with the relevant authorities before making personal arrangements.

Contents

List of illustrations

Preface to the Sixth Edition

Welcome to the writing business. You want to write, and you want to get your writing published, so where do you start?

First of all, let's get rid of the myth that publishing is a closed shop. It is not. You don't 'need to know someone to get in'. If you can offer quality work to the right market at the right time, you'll have as good a chance as anyone.

The writers who succeed are not always the most brilliant. They are the writers who provide what editors and publishers want. They write what people want to read.

In today's volatile and highly competitive publishing world, you need a guide to help you find your way to success. This book is your guide. Follow its advice and you'll save yourself a lot of time, money and frustration.

And remember this: we all start as beginners. Every writer whose name you recognise on bookshelves, in magazines and newspapers, in the theatre and on radio and television began, as you will begin, by sending out a first manuscript.

My aim is to show you how to get *your* work published. Believe me, and believe in yourself.

ACKNOWLEDGEMENTS

My thanks to these kind people who gave me permission to include copyright material: Alison Chisholm, Della Galton, Graham Lawler, Mike Pattinson, Iain Pattinson, Peggy Poole, Jean Saunders, D. C. Thomson & Co. Ltd, Steve Wetton and Stella Whitelaw.

AUTHOR'S NOTE

Editors and publishers, like writers, spring from both sexes. If anyone can invent a workable device to convey that fact neatly and without the awkward use of 'he or she', 'he/she', '(s)he' and the like, I'll be glad to hear from you. In the meantime, please read 'he', 'him' and 'his' throughout this text as embracing both men and women. No sexism is intended. After all, despite my slightly androgynous name, I am a woman.

Chriss McCallum

Getting Started

Writing for publication is a fiercely competitive business. Accept that fact at the outset, take a professional approach to both writing and marketing, and you'll increase your chances of success enormously.

In this chapter:

◆ what it takes to become a published writer
◆ basic equipment
◆ building your writer's reference library
◆ finding inspiration and support.

BEFORE YOU STEP IN

Publishing today is a buyers' market. You need to understand what that means for you, the beginning writer trying to break in. For example, the acceptance rate for novels submitted to the market is about one in two thousand – very long odds. But you *can* shorten them. You can:

◆ Get to know how the publishing world works.
◆ Learn how to identify, analyse and approach your target markets.
◆ Understand why you have to offer editors what they want, not what you think they *should* want.
◆ Learn how to develop a mutually profitable professional relationship with the editors and publishers you want to do business with.

The writing world is full of hopeful authors who will never see a word of theirs in print because they don't – or won't – understand the need to work at both the craft of writing and the art of selling.

There is no secret weapon, no magic formula. Success requires work – and staying power. Legions of writers bombard editorial offices with manuscripts that are badly structured, poorly written and all too often directed to the wrong markets. These writers are amazed and upset when their submissions boomerang home trailing rejection slips. Many give up in despair after only one or two tries.

You can succeed where these writers fail. You can learn:

◆ The basic techniques of good writing.
◆ How to structure your writing.
◆ How to choose and use language effectively.
◆ How to communicate your thoughts clearly, without muddle or ambiguity.
◆ How to capture and hold your reader's interest.
◆ How to revise and rewrite, and rewrite again until your work is as good as you can make it.

You'll find references throughout the following chapters to books, magazines, associations, services and information sources that will help you master the craft of writing and develop the marketing skills you need to become a published writer. To avoid unnecessary repetition, details are given in the appendices – titles, names, addresses, telephone numbers, e-mail and website addresses.

You'll also find advice and encouragement, and the occasional caution, all designed to help you achieve your goal.

Take yourself seriously ...

You might not find it easy to think of yourself as a serious writer when you're just starting out. You'll agonise about your chances of success and wake up in the small hours nagged by doubt. Take comfort. You are not alone – and beginners who are *too* sure of themselves tend to trip over their own egos.

Approach your writing in a professional manner from the start. Have confidence in your capacity to learn. After all, if you don't believe in your ability, how can you expect to convince other people.

... and be taken seriously

This book aims to help you build your confidence, judgement and credibility. It will also:

♦ Give you a working knowledge of the writing business and its accepted practices and conventions, to help you avoid many of the pitfalls that can trip up the inexperienced writer.

♦ Help you decide where you want to start. Even if you've already chosen your field (or if your field has chosen you, as often happens) don't dismiss other options without exploring them. You might see a more inviting path, or want to change direction later.

Common sense

Too many new writers are drawn to one of two extreme attitudes:

♦ There's the writer who devours all the advice he can get hold of, treating every word as gospel. He tears himself apart trying to adapt his style, approach, technique, marketing strategy ... because the advice he's reading this week contradicts what he read last week. He has no faith in his own judgement, and makes no effort to develop any.

♦ The opposite type refuses to consider *any* advice or help from anyone. He drives editors to distraction with his lack of common sense. He shoots off book-length manuscripts to tiny magazines, single poems to book publishers, erudite essays to mass-market magazines ...

— WISE WORDS —

Learn the business, use your common sense and you won't create problems where none need exist.

Here, then, are a few basic common-sense dos and don'ts to bear in mind:

1. *Do* study the techniques of good clear writing, but *don't* submerge your individuality.

2. *Do* study your markets so you send them material that is suitable, but *don't* copy their style and content so closely that you sacrifice every trace of originality.

3. *Do* be courteous and businesslike in all your dealings with editors, but *don't* regard them as either enemies or gods. They are not 'anti' new writers, or unapproachable, or infallible, or exalted – they are human beings with problems and prejudices, mortgages and falling hair, just like the rest of us.

4. *Do* work at cultivating your own judgement, but *don't* try to defy the conventions before you understand them.

5. And, above all, *do* write. *Don't* just think or talk or read or dream about writing. *Do it.*

BASIC EQUIPMENT

In theory, all you need is a pen and a pad of paper. That's fine, if you only want to target the 'Letters' or 'Tips' pages of magazines. Beyond that level, editors won't read handwritten scripts. You must be able to present your work in the form of a professional-looking word-processed print-out. Though it looks like a contradiction in terms, this is called a manuscript (abbreviation 'ms', plural 'mss').

You'll need:

◆ Pens and pocket-sized notebooks, so you can jot down ideas instantly. Keep one by your bed, too, to capture (in the dark if necessary) those verge-of-sleep flashes of brilliance. They'll be lost by morning if you don't. (A pocket tape recorder is even better.) Ideas, impressions, words, phrases, overheard comments and anecdotes – they can slip away forever if you don't pin them down.

◆ Plain white A4 (11.6 × 8.2 inches) paper, 80 gsm (grams per square metre) weight, for manuscripts. You need a decent quality that will stand up to a lot of handling and marking-up. Good copier paper is fine. (Don't waste this on notes or drafts – get cheap notepads and paper from cut-price stationery shops.)

- A decent printer. You need to be able to produce a sharp clear *black* print-out.

- Plain white DL size (9 × 4.5 inches) business envelopes.

- C5 (9 x 6.5 inches) envelopes to hold up to four A4 sheets folded once.

- A4 envelopes, to hold mss of more than four sheets without folding.

TIP

Mail-order companies and office supply shops are cheaper than high-street shops.

Unless you're rich, you'll need to prepare your manuscripts yourself. (Rates for professional computer word-processing are at least £3 per 1,000 words plus extra for hard copies, of which you'll need at least two – one to send out and one to keep in your files – plus a copy on disk.) Even a short novel could cost £300–£400, enough to buy a computer package nowadays.

As a writer with serious ambitions, it's essential that you invest in a good quality computer and printer set-up. More and more publications and book publishers now require material to be supplied on disk as well as on paper. You'll be at a considerable disadvantage, too, if you can't communicate with editors and send work by e-mail.

With a computer you can:

- Edit your work without retyping whole pages.
- Store electronic copies of everything you write.
- Print copies of your writing as and when you need them.
- Copy your work onto computer disks.
- Send files of your work anywhere in the world.
- Send query letters by e-mail.
- Respond to editors' questions in minutes rather than days.
- Find information via the Internet.

> **— WISE WORDS—**
>
> Learn to touch type, so you can concentrate on your writing, not on what your fingers are doing. Take a course, or buy Ann Dobson's book *Touch Typing in Ten Hours*.

Every successful writer works in his or her own way. Fay Weldon, interviewed on Channel 4, declared that if the day ever comes when she's required to write on a machine she'll stop writing. She writes with a pen and pad, and pays someone else to prepare her mss. That's fine, if you can afford the luxury.

> **— WISE WORDS—**
>
> A computer is only a tool. It can't create publishable work by itself – only you, the writer, can do the creating.

The golden rule
Always back up your work onto a separate disk at the end of every work session. Ideally, make copies on two disks and keep one on other premises, perhaps in your shed or garage, in case of – heaven forbid – fire or burglary.

Make backing up an unbreakable habit. Writers have lost weeks or even years of work because they haven't bothered to take this basic precaution.

BUILDING YOUR REFERENCE LIBRARY
Buy these books – you'll use them a lot:

♦ A big fat dictionary. *Chambers Dictionary* is excellent.

♦ The *latest* edition of the *Writers' & Artists' Yearbook* or *The Writer's Handbook*. Buy both if you can afford to. These annual directories list book, magazine and newspaper publishers, with details of what they want from writers, plus radio, stage and TV markets. The *Yearbook* gives lots of valuable advice about writing and getting published, agents, associations, services, plus information about tax liabilities, rights, copyright and so on. The *Handbook* lists fewer outlets than the *Yearbook* but gives more details about those it does include, and covers more radio, TV and stage outlets.

- The *New Oxford Dictionary for Writers and Editors*. For difficult spellings and usage, many proper names, capitalisation, abbreviations, foreign words and phrases.

- A concise encyclopaedia, like the annual *Pears Cyclopaedia*.

- *Roget's Thesaurus*, which lists synonyms for almost every word in the English language. Marvellous for finding just the right word – but don't get addicted.

Note: Other recommended books are listed in appropriate chapters throughout the book.

INFORMATION SOURCES

Using the public library

You'll probably use the library a good deal, so it's worth noting the main category divisions of the Dewey Decimal Classification System, which is used in most UK libraries. The category numbers are shown on the shelves, and it saves time if you know where to look:

000 General works
100 Philosophy
200 Religion
300 Social Sciences
400 Languages
500 Science
600 Technology
700 The arts and recreations
800 Literature
900 Geography, biography and history

The Internet

The World Wide Web offers infinite research resources. You can find information on any and every subject. Bear in mind, though, that anyone, whether individuals or companies, can publish anything they wish, so don't assume that everything you read is accurate and true. Unless you *know* your source is impeccable – like, for example, the British Library – double-check everything. Anyone can claim to be an expert on anything – *no one controls the Internet.*

We'll look in more detail about the advantages of the Internet in the next chapter.

Out-of-print books and books on your specialist subjects

The monthly *Book and Magazine Collector* lists books 'For Sale' and 'Wanted'. Although mainly meant for book dealers and collectors, it's useful for writers, too. Many book dealers specialise, and you can put your name on the mailing lists of those who deal in books relevant to your particular interests. You can advertise for books yourself, too. The magazine also carries ads for book-finding services.

Writers' magazines

There are magazines specially produced for writers. They print advice, news, reviews, competition notices, information on what's happening on the writing scene, plus author interviews and articles on the craft and business of writing and getting published.

Most writers' magazines are sold on subscription, but two are stocked by larger newsagents. These are:

◆ *Writing Magazine*, the glossy 'big sister' of the monthly subscription title *Writers' News* (see below), and supplied as part of the *Writers' News* subscription package. *Writing Magazine* carries articles and interviews offering advice and encouragement to writers at all levels, both hobby writers and professionals, and has market information, an 'agony' section, many regular columns, competitions, and a multitude of advertisements for writing, editorial and publishing services. The magazine is read by many established writers looking for new markets and wanting to keep up with what's happening in the writing world.

- *Writers' Forum*, an attractively produced monthly, available both on subscription and from large newsagents. Covering all aspects of writing and getting published, *Writers' Forum* also runs regular prose and poetry competitions, including competitions for young writers, and publishes the prize-winners.

If you want to offer work to markets in the United States, you'll find these magazines invaluable:

- *Writer's Digest*, an American bi-monthly packed with encouragement and information, taking a specifically commerce-oriented approach to writing and getting published.

- *The Writer*, another American title, also publishing advice and information, but aimed more towards the literary writer.

Subscription-only magazines include:

- *Writers' News*, the original monthly news magazine from the publishers of *Writing Magazine*. Carries news, advice, market information, a range of competitions and many ads for writers' services.

- *The New Writer*, published every two months, tending towards the 'creative/ literary' rather than hard 'how-to'. Publishes articles, opinion pieces and columns, poems and short fiction from subscribers only. Subscription now includes a regular e-mail newsletter.

- *Flair News*, a bi-monthly 32-page A5 magazine for subscribers to Flair for Words, a small friendly organisation offering critique services and advice to its members.

- *The Author* is the official quarterly magazine of the Society of Authors. Non-members can buy it on subscription – see the society's website.

There are many writers' e-zines (electronic magazines) published on the Internet. Many are freely accessible, and some publish poetry and short stories (see Chapter 2). There are also a number of electronic newsletters available, offering articles and advice on writing and getting published, plus up-to-date market information. Most of these are free to subscribers, being supported financially by advertising.

TIP
Writers' magazines help you to feel part of the writing community.

FINDING INSPIRATION AND SUPPORT

Writing can be a lonely business. Some writers prefer to work in isolation, but others need the stimulation of company to spark off ideas and exchange thoughts and views (and complaints about editors and agents). Once you start looking for kindred spirits, you'll be surprised how many you'll find around you.

Writers' circles

There might be a writers' group in your district, or at least close enough for you to attend occasionally. Your library should have contact details.

The National Association of Writers' Groups (NAWG) is a UK-wide organisation of writers' circles which produces a regular newsletter called *Link* and which holds an annual three-day conference. Individuals can join as associate members. (See under 'Associations Open to Unpublished Writers'.)

The *Directory of Writers' Circles, Courses and Workshops* is published twice a year and gives details of hundreds of writers' circles around the UK, including online postal groups and courses. Editor and publisher Diana Hayden offers free updates as information changes. (See under 'Recommended Reading.)

If you want face-to face contact with other writers but can't find a local group, why not start one yourself? A notice in the local paper (contact the editor) or pinned up in the library should turn up at least a fellow scribe or two. You could meet once or twice a month in each other's homes, or meet occasionally and keep in touch by telephone or e-mail. When you have enough members, you could hire a room regularly and share the cost.

Meeting other writers in a group can help in several ways. Members provide mutual support, encouragement and comfort when it's needed. You can share the cost of subscriptions to writers' magazines and build up a library of writers' manuals and reference books. Members can exchange publications for market study and club together to buy stationery in bulk.

Your local Arts Council office will advise about inviting guest speakers and help you to find them. Some Regional Arts Boards have schemes to help groups pay for visiting speakers.

Classes, seminars and residential courses
Most Local Education Authority (LEA) and Workers' Educational Association (WEA) syllabuses include 'Creative Writing' and are advertised in the local press before the start of each term. The library should also have information.

Seminars and courses are held countrywide throughout the year. They are advertised in writing magazines and circulated to writers' groups.

Writers who get involved in seminars and residential courses find that their enjoyment, enthusiasm and stimulation, and the friendships they form there, carry over into writing at home and keep them going when they might otherwise become discouraged.

Here are four of the best – see 'Useful Addresses' for contact details.

◆ The Arvon Foundation runs residential courses in Shropshire, West Yorkshire and Inverness-shire. Courses cover every kind of writing from poetry to novel-writing and journalism, with tutoring by top writers. You can get a brochure from the national administration office.

◆ The Writers' Summer School is held each August at the Hayes Conference Centre, Swanwick, Derbyshire. The oldest-established of the British writers' conferences, having run at the same venue since 1949, Swanwick offers five full days of concentrated advice on all aspects of writing. The programme includes formal lectures by leading figures in the writing and publishing world plus a choice of courses, workshops and talks throughout the week. Cost varies according to the accommodation you choose. Send an A5 stamped self-addressed envelope to the secretary. Application forms are sent out in late January and places get booked up quickly.

◆ The Writers' Holiday in Wales, at Caerleon, is another week-long writers' 'get-together', organised by Anne Hobbs in late July each year. Accommodation at Caerleon is in single student-type en-suite bedrooms in residential blocks. Reservations are accepted up to a year ahead against a small non-returnable deposit.

◆ The Winchester Writers' conference, held annually in late June/early July, offers competitions, mini-courses, workshops, seminars, talks and one-to-one sessions where writers can discuss their work with agents and editors.

Correspondence courses

The value of correspondence courses generates ongoing and often heated debate. One writers' magazine conducted a survey among its readers and found that success or failure appeared to depend almost entirely on the calibre of the tutors. The response from course students, past and current at the time of the survey, also indicated that the chances of a student being allocated a competent and helpful tutor are no more than 50-50. Students' comments ranged from 'my tutor was all I hoped for and more. I have recouped the cost of the course three times over' through 'kindly comments but very little constructive criticism' to 'worse than useless – some of the markets I was advised to send my work to no longer existed'.

It appears, too, that the only qualification needed to be appointed as a tutor is to be a 'published writer' – of what and how long ago doesn't seem to be an issue. Tutors are poorly paid in relation to the cost of the courses, so it seems reasonable to assume that, with a few honourable exceptions, they are unable or unwilling to spend much time on each student assignment. Success would appear to be as much a matter of luck, then, as of hard work on the student's part.

The student drop-out rate is high. According to information from several tutors, many students give up in the early stages, and a significant number do nothing at all after the first or second assignments, even if they've paid the full cost up front.

The bigger schools advertise widely in the national press, in consumer magazines, even on television, as well as in writers' magazines. Smaller enterprises confine their advertising to publications specifically aimed at writers. If you're thinking of signing up, hold off till you get on the information grapevine, and don't part with your hard-earned before you've seen references or had a personal recommendation.

— WISE WORDS—

Check credentials before you send money to advertisements for courses.

In a 1997 court case, a woman was jailed for six months and ordered to pay back £3,000 in compensation to 53 aspiring writers who responded to her ad for a writing course. The 'course' consisted of three handwritten paragraphs on finding work as a writer. Think about it: 53 people parted with more than £50 each without making *any* checks.

Your money might be better spent on a selection of writing manuals, or a couple of subscriptions to established writers' magazines, or attending a few seminars, or, if you can possibly afford it, a week's residential course.

There are courses available via the Internet, too. It's worth investigating the longer-established ones.

Writer's block
Before we go on to look at the various types of writing, let's strip the mystique from this much discussed 'affliction' about which whole books have been written.

Sometimes called 'frozen brain syndrome', writer's block does exist. Illness, bereavement, money troubles, for example, can all paralyse the creative spirit. All too often, though, 'the block' is a self-inflicted problem. You stare at the blank page. You *want* to write. You drink another cup of strong coffee. Still nothing comes. Why?

The reasons are seldom mysterious, muse-dependent or beyond your control. Ask yourself these questions:

Fiction

1. Do you really *want* to write fiction? Or do you equate 'being a writer' with 'being a short-story writer' or 'being a novelist'? (Be honest – you won't write anything well if your heart isn't in it.)

2. If you're certain that fiction *is* your field, have you taken time to think about your characters – what kind of people they are, what has made them that way, what they want, how they're likely to behave, how they'll react to and interact with each other in the situations you plan for them? Do you *know* them?

3. Have you prepared a convincing background for your story, from knowledge and experience and/or from research?

4. Have you experimented to find the right storytelling character and viewpoint?

5. Have you allowed time for your story to simmer, to build in your mind till it's boiling over and you can't wait another second to get it down on paper?

6. Or have you 'talked it to death' by discussing the story, the characters and the actions with your writers' group, your e-mail buddy or your family and friends? Few things will destroy your enthusiasm for a story faster than telling other people about it.

Non-fiction

1. Do you care about your subject? Does it move you, excite, annoy, thrill, disturb, infuriate, inspire you? Do you *really* have something to say about it?

2. Or did you choose it because it looked marketable? It didn't look too challenging? You were stuck for ideas? You don't care too much *what* you write as long as you write *something*?

3. Assuming you do have something to say, have you researched the subject thoroughly, and formulated your own ideas about it?

4. Have you at least roughed out a plan of the work?

In other words, are you trying to write something that's more of a chore than a pleasure, something you've talked all the energy out of, or something that is not yet ready to be written?

CHECKLIST FOR GETTING STARTED

1. Begin to learn about the writing process and the publishing business. Buy, or borrow from the library, the *latest* editions of the *Writers' & Artists' Yearbook* and *The Writer's Handbook* and read them from cover to cover.

2. If you can't type, take action to learn. Good keyboard skills will allow your brain to focus on *what* you're writing, not *how* you're writing it. If you're interested in writing for magazines and/or newspapers, consider learning shorthand, too; it's essential for aspiring journalists, and useful, too, for taking notes at interviews and seminars.

3. Join (or initiate) a writers' group. Enquire at the library. Advertise for other writers. Send for the *Directory of Writers' Circles, Courses and Workshops*.

4. Learn about the pleasures and problems you'll have in common with other writers. Subscribe to at least one writers' magazine.

Now you should know:

- What it takes to become a published writer.
- What basic equipment you need.
- What basic books you need.
- Where to find information.
- Where to find inspiration and support.

The Internet

We live in exciting times. Changes we couldn't have imagined even twenty years ago are happening now in our writing world. We have much to gain from the new technology. Don't be afraid of it. Welcome it, use it wisely, and you'll soon wonder how you managed without it. Remember, though, that the Internet is your tool, not your master.

In this chapter:

◆ what is the Internet?
◆ what is the World Wide Web?
◆ using e-mail
◆ blogging
◆ podcasting
◆ what might the future hold?

WHAT IS THE INTERNET?
Picture a worldwide network of interlinked computers capable of unlimited intercommunication and able both to store and to share information. This vast system is there for us to use, 24 hours a day, seven days a week. We can communicate with others and access information all over the world *without leaving our desks*.

There are no borders or boundaries in this electronic world. All you need is a computer, a connecting device called a modem and a service provider to whom you pay a regular access fee.

You can try out the Internet at many public libraries and 'cyber-cafés' but, believe me, you're going to want your own equipment.

Accessing the Internet

You need to subscribe to an Internet Service Provider (ISP). There are several magazines giving information about ISPs, their services and charges. Check them out before you commit yourself, or ask Internet-savvy friends for recommendations.

TIP

Many ISPs offer free 'no commitment' trial periods and some offer free or very cheap access when you sign up. Be wary of the latter if you're a novice – their helplines can be *very* expensive. ISPs whose fees include online and telephone help facilities can be more cost-effective.

WHAT IS THE WORLD WIDE WEB?

The two functions of the Internet of most use to writers are the World Wide Web and e-mail (see below).

The World Wide Web (abbreviation www) is a super-huge collection of websites. Each website is a collection of pages linked together under a single domain name, a URL (Unique Reference Locator). Each URL address begins with the protocol http:// usually (though not invariably) followed by www., then the specific domain address. Don't be put off by the long strings of letters and symbols that make up web addresses. In practice, the http:// prefix is rapidly becoming a 'given' and is being omitted from printed addresses.

To access a website, you first sign on with your ISP, then call up a search engine, an electronic catalogue. You then key your target URL into the address box, click on a small box alongside it marked 'Search' or 'Go' or 'Find' or something similar. This activates your search engine, which then combs hundreds of millions of pages across the web to find the address you want – in a breathtakingly few seconds.

URLs *must* be keyed in accurately. Even a single wrong letter or symbol will make your request unrecognisable. Life is getting a lot easier, though, as most search engines now let us ask for the address in normal language. (Key in, for example, 'UK publishers' and marvel at the number of relevant websites listed on your screen.)

The World Wide Web works on the principle of universal ownership: *anyone anywhere* can access all the information published there.

DID YOU KNOW?
You can read newspapers published anywhere in the world, with a few clicks of your mouse.

The web opens up a marvellous range of information and resources:

♦ **Research**. You can find information on any and every subject. Bear in mind, though, that anyone, whether individuals or companies, can publish anything they wish so, unless you *know* your source is impeccable, double-check everything. Anyone can claim to be an expert on anything – *no one controls the Internet.*

> **— WISE WORDS —**
>
> Be wary of self-styled experts.

♦ **Markets**. Many magazines now publish online editions, and some show writers' guidelines for their print editions, too. You can also check out publishers' catalogues worldwide.

♦ **Links**. Nearly every writing website, whatever its topic, offers links to other relevant websites. Links typically appear in underlined blue type. A click on the underlined words calls up the linked website. It's as easy as that. It's also pretty easy to lose track of where you've come from, so if you find a website you particularly like and might want to revisit, you can 'bookmark' the site.

You can also get involved, if you wish, with online writers' communities and 'chat rooms', where you can 'meet' other writers with similar interests. You could find a writing 'buddy' anywhere in the world.

◆ **E-zines**. Also called webzines, these are online Small-Press-type magazines that might also be produced in a print version. Most are freely accessible, some ask for a subscription. Some are available to read on-screen, others are sent by e-mail. There are e-zines publishing every topic imaginable, some on subjects so esoteric they couldn't survive in print but can be produced on the web at very little cost, to the delight of their devotees.

There are also hundreds of e-zines about writing and the writing life, easily found via links in 'writing' websites. To read some e-zines, you might need a facility called Adobe Acrobat Reader, which is free to download from the Adobe website (www.adobe.com).

◆ **Your own website**. You can set up your own website to promote yourself, displaying examples of your work (provided you still hold the copyright), your CV and any services you want to offer. Most ISPs offer web space where you can set up your own pages as part of your subscription deal.

◆ **Other people's websites**. Many writers with established websites offer other writers the chance to promote themselves, or provide links to their websites, as a mutual deal or possibly for a small fee.

◆ **Your own blog**. It's easy to set up your own web-log, universally called a blog. A blog is an online diary that you regularly update with entries, called 'posts', on any topic you choose to write about. You can tell the world about your writing, post examples, invite comments and expand your online presence for very little financial outlay. In his wonderfully simple guide to blogging, *Blog Wild!*, American writer Andy Wibbels (www.goblogwild.com) defines the blog as 'an easily, instantly and frequently updated web site, focused around a topic, industry or personality'. Most ISPs provide facilities for you to set up a blog.

◆ **Podcasting**. A podcast is an online broadcast. With a computer, an Internet connection and a microphone you can broadcast to the world. See Wikipedia for a detailed explanation, or read a book like Steve Shipside's *Podcasting – The Ultimate Starter Kit*, which includes a start-up CD.

Beware Internet sharks

The Internet equivalent of the vanity publisher, these predators advertise widely in writers' magazines – and their promises sound wonderfully convincing. They offer to post your work on their website – for a fee – and assure you that every agent and editor in the world is eager to read what you've written. Don't fall for this. Agents' and publishers' desks groan under piles of work waiting to be read. Manuscripts lie in heaps on their floors. More arrive every working day and there is never enough time to read them all. Where is the logic in claiming that these busy people want to trawl the web for undiscovered talent?

RED LIGHT

Internet sharks will tempt you with offers to display your work on a website, usually at considerable expense, '... so that publishers and agents searching for new talent can read your novel, screenplay, poetry, short stories.'

One such company used the name of a well known agent in their advertising material without permission. Asked to comment on this at a Society of Authors' meeting, this agent dismissed the claim that editors or agents would seek material in this way as 'Absolute b**ls**t.'

USING E-MAIL

One of the most useful aspects of the Internet is the facility to send and receive e-mail (electronic mail). It's fast and cheap, and it doesn't intrude at inconvenient times.

Most ISPs allow you up to seven password-controlled e-mail addresses for sending and receiving e-mail. This can be particularly useful for writers who use pen names.

With e-mail you can:

◆ Write your e-mails offline and have them sent out at a time of your choosing.
◆ Keep an electronic address book of contacts.

- Send the same message to any number of people at the same time.
- Keep copies of all messages sent and received.
- Sign up to receive appropriate newsletters, delivered regularly (and usually free) to any of your password-controlled addresses.
- Send queries to editors (see below).
- Deal with corrections and updates quickly and easily.

Sending queries by e-mail

E-mail queries are becoming increasingly popular. In the US, for example, about 90 per cent of all queries are now sent this way. Receiving, assessing and replying to queries is faster and therefore more efficient than by post. This can be particularly useful when you're working to tight deadlines. It's also a great boon when the mail deliveries are disrupted by, for example, strike action.

E-mail queries demand different tactics from conventional paper queries. Here are a few tips to help you get it right:

1. Before you contact any editor, find out if they welcome e-mail queries. It's pointless to send queries this way if they're never going to be read. Some editors still prefer queries on paper. It's up to you to find out the preferred approach. The information you need might be in the reference books or on the publication's website. If not, check by making a *brief* phone call to the editorial department. Check for a special e-mail address for queries.

2. Don't let the technology distract you from the purpose of your query. Your aim is the same as if you were sending a conventional query: to persuade the editor you have a great idea that is just right for their publication and you are the ideal person to write it.

3. Take great care over the wording of your subject line. You need to make sure the purpose of the e-mail is clear and unambiguous. Every e-mail address these days is inundated with 'spam', uninvited messages advertising everything from sex aids to get-rich-quick scams. Don't try to be smart or 'intriguing' by writing a teasing subject line. Avoid words like 'free', 'offer', 'benefit', 'urgent', 'unique' and the like. Such words could trigger the ISP's

'spam alert', and could risk instant deletion, *unread*. Start with 'Query', then be brief and to the point. For example, 'Query for your Current Affairs section', or 'Query for Mary Smith, Homes Department' should at least get your query looked at.

4. Don't be over-familiar or chatty. The ease of e-mail communication tends to encourage informality. Resist this. You won't impress any editor with 'Hi, Mary' or 'Today's your lucky day, Joe'. Word your e-mail query as courteously as you would a letter. Craft it carefully, too, and set it out logically. You want to send a subliminal message that any work they show interest in will be done with integrity and delivered on time.

5. Take care with spelling and punctuation. Don't spoil the impression of care and efficiency with sloppy English or careless punctuation.

6. Remember to include *all* your contact information: telephone number, fax number if you have one and your postal address as well as your e-mail address. Make it as easy as possible for the editor to contact you.

7. Don't overload your query with information. If you have publishing credits relevant to your query, mention these in a brief paragraph at the end. Offer to send samples on request and have photocopies ready to send if they're asked for. *Do not* send attachments with your query. Many editors won't open e-mails with attachments unless they've been requested from people they know, because they fear their systems might be contaminated by viruses.

8. Don't expect a reply by return. The editor needs time to consider your query. Don't bombard his mail box with follow-up e-mails demanding a decision – he might get fed up with you and hit the delete key.

RED LIGHT
Never send attachments unless and until they're requested.

THE FUTURE

Jason Epstein, former editorial director of Random House and co-founder of the *New York Review of Books*, writes in his memoir *Book Business – Publishing Past,*

Present and Future that in his opinion reading on screen may never be the major mode of distribution for books. He believes it highly likely 'that most digital files will be printed and bound on demand at point of sale by machines ... which within minutes will inexpensively make single copies that are indistinguishable from books made in factories.'

Imagine that – pop into a café, select a book from a catalogue on the ATM-like machine in the corner, pay with your debit card, and by the time you've had your cappuccino your book will be ready to collect. Whether you find that prospect exciting or depressing, it could be the future of mass-market books.

The technology is already being tried in the US, with some reports of unsatisfactory binding, loose pages and the like. However, all new technologies have teething problems, and you can be sure these will be sorted out.

The costliest part of the bookselling business is the warehousing and distribution of books. Already many authors are bypassing publishing companies as we know them and publishing their books themselves, either on the Internet or by 'print on demand' technology. Neither of these methods requires the storage of large quantities of books. We'll look at these options in Chapter 14.

Recommended reading
Richard Quick, *Web Design in Easy Steps.*
Steve Shipside, *Podcasting – The Ultimate Starter Kit.*
Andy Wibbels, *Blog Wild!*

Now you should know:

◆ What the Internet and the World Wide Web are and how they work.
◆ What e-mail is and how it can help writers.
◆ How to make sure your e-query gets read.
◆ What blogging is.
◆ What podcasting is.
◆ Some of the current and future advantages for writers.

3

Understanding Rights and Contracts

To safeguard your own rights and to ensure that you don't infringe the rights of others, you need a basic working knowledge of how the law protects intellectual property.

In this chapter:

◆ copyright
◆ moral rights
◆ plagiarism
◆ libel
◆ rights in book writing
◆ rights in magazine and newspaper writing
◆ electronic rights
◆ co-authorship
◆ Public Lending Right.

COPYRIGHT

Copyright simply means 'the right to copy'. No one has the right to reproduce, print, publish or sell any part of your writing without your permission. The law protects your copyright during your lifetime and for 70 years after your death. Your copyright is your intellectual property; you can sell it outright if you wish, but you would then have no further claim on that work or on any money made from it.

> *DID YOU KNOW?*
> Copyright protects personal letters – the *letter* belongs to the recipient, but the *words* belong to the writer.

In the UK, you don't have to register copyright. It's yours the minute you set your words down on paper.

The copyright line you see in books and magazines – the symbol © followed by the copyright holder's name – warns that the work is protected. You don't have to put this line on your ms. Your work is automatically protected at law.

> — **WISE WORDS** —
>
> Although it seldom happens, if you really are worried that someone might 'steal' your work, it's easy to protect yourself. Send a copy of the work to yourself by registered post, then deposit the *unopened* package and your dated receipt in a bank or with your solicitor. Get a dated receipt there as well.

If you're tempted to sell your copyright ...

You might be asked to sell your material outright, including the copyright, for a fixed one-off payment. Don't do this, even if the wolf has two feet inside your door. You might be signing away a fortune.

DID YOU KNOW?

When the von Trapp family fled to America as the Nazis occupied Europe, they sold all the rights in their story, including the copyright, for the price of a few weeks' food and lodging. Their story became the multi-million-dollar musical *The Sound of Music*. The von Trapps never saw a cent of that money.

The copyright laws work both ways

Just as your work is protected from other writers' plundering, *you* can't quote any substantial part of another writer's work without written permission. And that permission can be expensive. (See *The Writer's Handbook* for current quotation fees.) Permission to use copyright material should be sought from the publishers of that material, and fees can vary from publisher to publisher.

MORAL RIGHTS

The provision of 'moral rights', meaning the rights of 'paternity' and 'integrity', was introduced in the 1988 Copyright, Designs and Patents Act.

The right of paternity is the author's right to be clearly identified as the creator of a work. The right of integrity is the author's right to prevent any distortion or mutilation of his work that would damage his reputation.

The 1988 Act requires the UK author to assert his moral rights in writing. You'll see such a notice in the prelims of most books published since 1988.

Moral rights are separate from copyright. The 1988 Act provides for the waiving of moral rights. Some magazine and newspaper publishers try to insist that writers waive their moral rights, perhaps implying that such a waiver is a condition of acceptance. Writers are vigorously resisting this. If you're faced with this dilemma, do take legal advice.

'Fair dealing'
This rather vague term describes the legitimate use of published material 'for purposes of criticism or review'. This is generally interpreted to mean that you can quote a line or two to illustrate a point you want to make, *provided you give due acknowledgement of the source of the quotation.*

If you want to quote at length, however, or display a substantial quotation in a prominent position in your own work, you would be wise to seek permission. See, for example, page 140, where a page of Steve Wetton's material is reproduced to show how to set out a playscript. I would have no right to use such a substantial extract without Steve's express permission.

Until you're clear about the legal niceties, you would be safer either to avoid quoting from other writers' work altogether or to seek permission for *anything* you want to quote.

PLAGIARISM
Plagiarism is the use without permission of work in which the copyright is held by someone else. You could hit problems if, for example, you were to follow someone else's storyline too closely, or incorporate parts of someone else's work into your own.

You might remember the gaffe made by Princess Michael of Kent when she wrote her book *Crowned in a Far Country*. She included large chunks of other authors' works without acknowledgement and was publicly criticised for this.

DID YOU KNOW?

In 1987, the Estate of Margaret Mitchell brought a complaint of plagiarism against French author Régine Desforges. Mme Desforges's novel trilogy (published in Britain as *The Blue Bicycle* trilogy) is an obvious re-telling of *Gone With the Wind* in a Second World War setting. The plot and the principal characters have much more than a passing resemblance to those of the famous American Civil War novel, and Mme Desforges did not deny that the American novel provided the inspiration for the trilogy. She was sued nevertheless, lost her case and was heavily fined.

Be wary of titles, too. Although there's no copyright on titles, you could have problems if you called your novel *Atonement* or *The Da Vinci Code*. This could be seen as a deliberate attempt to mislead.

LIBEL

Libel is a statement made in writing or in print, or broadcast in any medium, which defames the character of an identifiable living person by holding them up to ridicule or contempt.

Don't be caught out by an unintentional libel. If you make recognisable use, for instance, of a public figure (or even your neighbour) as the model for a character who commits a criminal act or is portrayed as a 'baddie', you could be sued.

The same caution applies to the use of names. You could find yourself in trouble if you create a villain who holds, for example, a specific position in a company and who bears the same name as a person in such a position in real life. Check such names with sources like company registers. Take care, too, with company names. If your novel features, for example, a jeweller's shop where someone knowingly acts as a fence for stolen goods, make sure there's no real-life jeweller trading under that name.

CONTRACTS AND RIGHTS IN BOOK WRITING

When a publisher accepts your novel or commissions your non-fiction book, he will ask you to sign a contract. This document will have many clauses and sub-clauses, and might look dauntingly long and complex. Don't be afraid to ask for clarification or explanation. It's in your own interest to be clear about what you're signing.

RED LIGHT

Don't sign *anything* you're not sure you understand.

Contracts vary from publisher to publisher. To show you a specific contract could be misleading or confusing but, basically, this is what a book contract should include:

1. The date of the agreement, the names and addresses of the publisher and the author, and the title of the book – possibly a working title at this stage.

2. The author's obligations.

3. The publisher's obligations.

4. Detailed specification of rights assigned.

5. Provision for revised editions.

6. Specification of royalty.

7. Specification of accounting periods.

8. Warranties and indemnities.

9. Termination and reversion of rights.

10. Miscellaneous sub-clauses pertinent to the particular agreement negotiated.

Subsidiary rights

Scrutinise the small print before you sign. If you've written the kind of book that might attract, for example, film studios or product merchandisers (think *Star Trek*, *Harry Potter*, *Postman Pat*) make sure you're getting a fair deal.

Many a fortune has been lost to authors through unwise assignation of rights.

Subsidiary rights include, for example:

- Anthology and quotation rights.
- Condensation rights – magazines and books.
- TV, radio and recorded readings.
- Merchandising.
- Large-print editions.
- Electronic rights (see below).

The *offer* of a contract entitles you to approach the Society of Authors for membership. They will vet the document for you *before you sign it*. As agent Carole Blake says in her excellent book *From Pitch to Publication*, 'Your publishing contract is pivotal to your career. It's also vital to your bank balance: without one you'll not get paid!'

TIP
If you don't yet have an agent, you might want to approach one *before you sign*. The offer of a contract makes you a lot more attractive as a client, and an agent might be able to negotiate better terms for you.

RIGHTS IN WRITING FOR MAGAZINES AND NEWSPAPERS

Agreements in writing for magazines and newspapers are much shorter and usually less formal than those for books. Your contract might be no more than a letter or e-mail stating the terms agreed: wordage, delivery date, terms of payment and so on.

If the agreement is made by telephone, send the editor a dated letter or e-mail recording the conversation and keep printed copies so there are no doubts about what was agreed. It's important to do this because by the time your payment is due the editor might have forgotten the conversation or might even have left. A printed and dated record avoids confusion or argument.

It isn't necessary to put 'FBSR' (First British Serial Rights) in your covering letter or on your manuscript. The editor will assume that you're offering the right to publish the work for the first time and once only, unless you tell him otherwise. The payment you receive will be a single payment for a single use.

RED LIGHT

When your payment arrives, you might be asked to sign a note on the back of the cheque granting the publication the copyright in the work they're paying for. This is a try-on. Cross out the note *without signing*. Don't worry – payment will not be stopped, and it's highly unlikely that the publication will refuse to work with you again.

ELECTRONIC RIGHTS

With the rapid spread of electronic publishing via the Internet, many publishers now include electronic rights in the contract, whether or not they intend to exploit those rights.

You would be wise to hold on to the electronic rights in a work that has future potential as an electronic publication. While few e-publishers are yet making the predicted squillions of dollars, euros or pounds, electronic publishing is a young medium and the future is unpredictable.

Many rights problems are similar to those of conventional publishing. Although most material published on the Internet can be accessed and read free of any charges beyond your provider's fees, the same restrictions apply to its use, copying or exploitation as apply to printed material.

The Society of Authors publishes a useful *Quick Guide to Electronic Publishing Contracts*. Like all the society's Quick Guides, it's free to members and available for non-members to buy post-free.

CO-AUTHORSHIP

The law protecting copyright for a specified period after an author's death also covers writing partnerships, such as an artist collaborating with an author to produce an illustrated book, a lyric writer and a composer pooling their talents to write a song, two authors co-writing a book and so on. The work concerned does not come out of copyright and into the public domain – that is, free for anyone to use – until the full period of 70 years from the end of the calendar year in which *the last surviving partner* died.

Don't make the mistake of assuming that because one half of a writing team has been dead for the statutory period their work is automatically out of copyright. There was an expensive example of this error in the 1960s (when the statutory period of protection was 50 years) involving the partnership of Gilbert and Sullivan, who wrote the Savoy operas. Pye records made a jazz album titled *The Coolest Mikado*, based on Sir Arthur Sullivan's music for *The Mikado*. Pye released the record in 1961, but were obliged to withdraw it almost immediately at a huge financial loss. (If you come across one of the copies sold before the ban, it's a collector's item.)

Sullivan had died in 1900, so his 50-years-after-death period was long past. But W. S. Gilbert didn't die till 1911. The jazz arrangements were written and the recording made before Gilbert's copyright ran out, and his copyright protected Sullivan's music. Pye had infringed the joint copyright, and paid dearly for the mistake.

PUBLIC LENDING RIGHT

Public Lending Right (PLR) is a system under which publicly funded payment is made to authors whose books are lent by public libraries. Payment is made once a year and is proportionate to the number of times a book is borrowed based on figures from a sample of libraries.

As soon as you have a full-length book of any kind published, register it with the Public Lending Right Office. Send for a registration form or download the form from the PLR website.

Recommended reading

Carole Blake, *From Pitch to Publication*.

Michael Legat, *Understanding Publishers' Contracts*.

Helen Shay, *Writers' Guide to Copyright and Law*.

Society of Authors, *Quick Guide to Copyright and Moral Rights*.

Society of Authors, *Quick Guide to Electronic Publishing Contracts*.

Society of Authors, *Quick Guide to Publishing Contracts*.

Now you should know:

* How copyright and moral rights work.
* How to avoid plagiarism and libel.
* How to handle publishing contracts.
* How to handle magazine and newspaper contracts.
* What co-authorship rights mean.
* When to register your book for Public Lending Right.
* Where to find more information.

4

Keeping Records

Keep simple records of everything relevant to your writing business from the day you start. In particular, keep records of all your financial dealings, so you can submit accurate data to the Inland Revenue at the end of each tax year.

In this chapter:

- keeping track of submissions
- keeping a markets book
- keeping a 'writing only' diary
- recording income and expenditure
- tax-allowable expenses
- handling self-assessment.

KEEPING TRACK OF SUBMISSIONS

Use a record book with pages wide enough to note every submission: when and where you send it, whether it's accepted or rejected, paid for or not, and so on. You can use a spreadsheet on your computer if you wish, but it's a good idea to keep a record book as well – it can be more convenient for looking up the odd piece of data.

Item: Short story	*Title*: 'Star Struck'		*Length*: 1,500 words	
Date sent	*Sent to*	*Accepted/rejected*	*Payment received*	*Date*
25.01.200X	*Fiction Feast*	Rejected		17.03.200X
23.03.200X	*Dream On*	Accepted	£120	16.09.200X

Figure 1. Example of a submissions book.

Keep a page for each item you submit. You need to know what's happening to every article, story or poem you send out.

KEEPING A MARKETS BOOK

A loose-leaf A4 book gives you plenty of space, and lets you discard out-of-date pages. Keep records of information about individual markets, one market to a page, and note every item you send to that market. For each market note:

1. Information gathered – a précis of your market study – updated as and when changes happen.

2. Every item you send there, with a record of its progress.

3. Your experiences with this market – whether the staff are friendly or offhand, their responses prompt or slow, efficient or not, and so on.

4. Changes of personnel, editorial policy and the like.

5. Anything that might be useful for the future (even if it's only 'Never again!').

— WISE WORDS —

The markets get more and more volatile. Keep your market study up to date.

Dream On 11 Milky Way Starville XX7 7ZZ	Editor: Verity Verruca				
Date sent	Item	Accepted/ Rejected	Pay	Date	Remarks
03.04.200X	Short story 'Star Struck'	Accepted	£120	16.09.0X	Slow response but great to work with!

Figure 2. Example of a markets book.

KEEPING A 'WRITING ONLY' DIARY

Keep a separate diary to note, for example:

◆ Deadlines for submissions of commissioned work.
◆ Dates for submitting seasonal/anniversary material.

- ◆ Closing dates for competition entries.
- ◆ Writers' circle meetings.
- ◆ Other writers' events you plan to attend.

You might prefer a set of labelled folders, or some kind of electronic record. Whatever your method, keep it up to date.

> **— WISE WORDS —**
>
> Don't forget to cross-reference your writing diary with your social diary.

RECORDING INCOME AND EXPENDITURE

Any money legitimately spent on your writing business could be tax-deductible against earnings (see below).

By law you must declare *everything* you earn, however modest, in each financial year. The only exception *at the time of writing* is that competition prizes are not taxable. It's important, therefore, to note every penny you spend – the Inland Revenue doesn't like approximations or guesses.

Outgoing 200X			Incoming 200X		
June	£	p	*June*		£ p
1 Black cartridge 41645	24.35		9	'Top Tip' + photo	
Paperclips	0.99			(Gossip mag)	25.00
5 reams white A4 paper					
(John Jotter Ltd)	15.25		21	Article (Snob Gazette)	75.00
11 Photocopying					
('Bees' article)	0.40				
14 Book: 'Break into Print'					
(Bookbuff Ltd)	12.95				

Figure 3. Two facing pages of a cash book.

> **— WISE WORDS —**
>
> Keep all receipts relevant to your writing business – you could be asked to produce them.

If you spend a lot on postage – and most writers still do, even with increasing use of e-mail – keep a separate postage book. Enter purchases of stamps and International Reply Coupons (IRCs) in your cash book, and log each item posted, with destination, date of posting, stamps used and so on. In this way, you'll have to account (to yourself) for every stamp or IRC you use, so you won't be tempted to raid your 'writing' stamps for personal letters.

TAX-ALLOWABLE EXPENSES

Get a copy of the relevant Inland Revenue leaflet, available from the Inland Revenue website.

Keep all your dealings with the Inland Revenue as open and honest as possible from day one. It doesn't matter how sparse your earnings are, you're required to declare them.

The Inland Revenue allows you to set certain expenses against tax. You need to keep all relevant receipts as well as making detailed contemporaneous notes of expenditure in a diary or record book.

TIP

If you keep your records on a computer, you still need to keep the relevant paper records, receipts and so on.

Allowable expenses are those incurred wholly and exclusively for business purposes. The Inland Revenue makes distinctions between 'capital allowances' (equipment like personal computers, fax machines, photocopiers, etc.) and 'expenses' (outlay incurred in the day-to-day running of your writing business).

Expenses can include:

- Secretarial – typing, proofreading, researching, indexing, etc.
- Stationery – paper, envelopes, pens and pencils, file cards, right down to small items like paper clips and staples.
- Postage.
- Telephone calls.
- Internet subscriptions.
- Subscriptions to periodicals relevant to your business.
- Maintenance of equipment used in your business, including computer supplies, software, batteries, etc.
- Travel at home and abroad for meetings with publishers, interviews, research and so on, including hotels and motoring expenses.
- Photocopying.
- Photography relevant to your business.
- Subscriptions to relevant societies and associations.
- Accountancy and legal charges incurred solely in the course of your writing business.
- TV and video rental, cinema and theatre tickets if solely for the purposes of your writing business.
- Office rental.
- If you work from home, an appropriate proportion of room use, heating, lighting and so on – but do take advice on this, as it could affect your home's exemption from certain tax liabilities.

Your tax liability is based on your net profit for the accounting year ending in the year of assessment. Take professional advice on the most appropriate date to choose as the end of your tax year. The Society of Authors can recommend reliable accountancy companies experienced in handling authors' tax affairs.

DID YOU KNOW?
The Inland Revenue has the absolute right to investigate your business for no specific reason and you will be billed for the cost. You might consider insuring against this. There are specialist schemes available – take advice from an accountant.

HANDLING SELF-ASSESSMENT

Unless you can afford to employ a professional accountant, you must deal with your tax return yourself. There is ample advice available on the Inland Revenue website.

Recommended reading

Society of Authors, *Quick Guide to Income Tax*.
Writers' & Artists' Yearbook, 'Finance' section.

Now you should know:

- How to keep track of all your submissions.
- How to keep financial records.
- Where to find information on income tax liabilities and self-assessment.

5

Preparing Your Work for Submission

Your submission says a lot about *you*. When you give an editor a crisp, clean, well set-out manuscript, with accurate spelling, grammar and punctuation, you encourage him to have confidence in its content, even before he reads it. You've shown him you care about what you're doing, and that you're approaching the job in a professional way. Even if he turns down *this* offering, you'll have banked some goodwill for the future.

In this chapter:

- preparing a prose manuscript
- dealing with illustrations
- selecting and studying a suitable market
- how agents work.

PREPARING A PROSE MANUSCRIPT

Always follow the accepted standard layout when you're typing short stories, articles or books. (See the relevant chapters for poetry, play-script and picture-script layouts.)

— WISE WORDS —

A well-presented manuscript could increase your chances of acceptance. A slovenly one could destroy them.

First impressions count

Editors dislike sloppy presentation. Don't imagine they'll toil through a scruffy script, ignoring coffee stains, cramped margins or eye-straining pages from an ink-starved printer in a tireless quest to find a new literary genius. They won't.

They might not read it at all.

You're offering your work for sale in a highly competitive market. Don't turn your customers off with tatty packaging.

Don't rush it. When you've done a complete draft, print it out – you'll see mistakes more easily on a printed page than on-screen. Then take time to:

♦ Check your spelling, grammar, punctuation and syntax.

♦ Alter any clumsy phrasing or repetitions and the like.

♦ Check that all personal and place names and descriptions are accurate and consistent.

♦ Check *any* facts you're not absolutely sure about. If an editor picks up even a tiny factual inaccuracy, he'll worry in case there's a big one somewhere.

♦ Finally, check the word count – see below. You should be working with a particular market in mind. Check *now* whether you need to cut any excess wordage.

TIP
When you've read each page, read it again line by line *from the bottom up*, covering the lines you've checked as you go. This is a proofreader's trick that throws up faults you can easily miss in a straight reading, where you tend to see what you expect to see.

Calculating your wordage

For an article or short story for a magazine, count every word and round up to the nearest ten. As most magazines are set in columns, there is little white space left at the paragraph ends, so you need an accurate count.

Books are different. Look at the text of any novel, for example. While most of the lines occupy the full width of the text area, many do not. Take lines like:

She looked up.
'Oh no,' she sighed.
'It's true.'

Here you have just nine words – and they use up three lines.

You'll get a distorted picture if you simply count words. (Computer word counts don't take short lines into account.) Treat every line, however short, as a full line, including the last lines of paragraphs.

This is how to do it:

1. Count the exact number of words in five sets of ten *full* lines picked at random throughout the text. Add up these five sets of numbers. Divide the total by 50. This gives the average number of words per line.

2. Add up the total number of lines in your ms, treating every line as a full line. With a reasonably consistent number of lines per page, you can multiply the total number of pages by the average number of lines per page.

3. Multiply the total number of lines by the average number of words per line.

Here's an example:

Total number of words in 50 full lines	=	710
Average number of words per line = 710/50	=	14.2
Total number of pages in the ms	=	193
Average number of lines per page	=	28
Total number of lines in the ms = 193×28	=	5,404
Total number of words = $5,404 \times 14.2$	=	76,736.8

Rounded up to the nearest thousand, your final word count, the figure you would put on your ms, would be 'About 77,000 words'.

Make it beautiful

Present your work like a professional:

◆ Use good quality plain white A4 paper. Your ms will have to stand up to a lot of handling and editorial marking.

◆ Your printer needs to be good enough to produce a clear, sharp, easy-to-read print-out. Use only *black* ink, and replenish it before it begins to run out.

◆ Avoid fancy typefaces (Gothic, italic, script and so on). And however keen you are to save paper, *never* use a condensed type. Choose a typeface that's as plain and easy on the eye as possible, like Times New Roman or Courier.

◆ Leave good margins all round, at least an inch, with a bit more on the left to accommodate typesetting instructions. Keep your pages uniform in layout.

◆ Set your paragraph format to double line spacing. That means leaving one *full* line of blank space between lines of type. It *does not mean* leaving a half line of space, and it *does not mean* hitting the space bar twice between words.

◆ To indicate a break in the action in a short story or novel, or to indicate sections in a non-fiction piece, leave an extra line space and start the first line of the next paragraph full out to the left margin, with no indent. Otherwise, don't leave extra space between paragraphs, but do indent the first line of each paragraph so that it's clear where the paragraphs begin and end.

◆ *Do not justify* (make even) the right-hand edge of your text. Leave this edge ragged.

◆ Don't underline *anything* unless you intend it to appear in italics.

Identify your work

Put your name and address on your cover sheet and on the first and last pages of text. Number the pages consecutively, even for a full-length work – *don't* begin again with 'Page 1' at the beginning of each chapter.

In your 'Header', type your name, the title (or an abbreviation of it) and insert the page numbers at top right. This gives you a strap-line, to ensure your pages don't get out of order (or mislaid).

Follow the layout as shown in Figure 4.

It really is essential to stick to the conventional forms of manuscript layout. These haven't come about by chance or been chosen at random. They're the layouts publishers and printers have found to be the clearest, quickest, safest and least expensive to work on:

◆ clearest because the double-spaced lines of plain black type on white paper are easy to read and less tiring to copyeditors' and typesetters' eyes;

◆ quickest because the wide margins and double-spaced text leave room for editorial corrections and typesetting instructions to be marked quickly and clearly, and also because they speed length calculations;

◆ safest because their clarity reduces the risk of typesetting errors or misunderstandings, even after corrections have been marked;

◆ least expensive because all the foregoing points contribute to speed and accuracy, cutting time-schedules and reducing the need for corrections at proof stage – helping to keep costs down and quality high.

— WISE WORDS—

Observing professional layouts will enhance your credibility.

The cover sheet

The cover sheet for the story in Figure 4 would look something like that shown in Figure 5. The layout can be varied, but you must show all the necessary information.

Short story   Chriss McCallum
750 words   3 The Birches
                                                     Rowan Town
                                                     Nutwoodshire
                                                     ZZ99 7AA
                                                     Tel: 0101 10 0110
                                                     E-mail: cmc@nut.net

Make Me an Offer

by Chriss McCallum

The men on the doorstep were strangers. Not that Charley expected to see anyone he knew. He wasn't unsociable. He enjoyed company as much as the next man, but he never encouraged visitors.

They were well dressed, smart in dark suits. One was small, thin and neat, ferrety, with eyes as black as boot buttons. A pearl tie-pin speared his silk tie. The other man was younger, pug-faced, and a lot bigger. They were friendly and polite, but they didn't fool Charley. He began to close the door, but the big man was already shoving a beefy shoulder into the gap.

Ferret-face smiled and went straight into the old routine.

'... Anything old, anything interesting. Top prices, of course ... old-established firm ... any good pieces ... curios, furniture, quality items ... Hard to find good stock these days. Happy to give you a valuation, sir. No obligation, of course.'

Of course.

Charley thought about telling them to push off, but the heavy shoulder was learning harder. He wouldn't get rid of them that easily. At his age, physical force was out, and his nearest neighbour was well out of shouting range. And it was getting dark.

He stepped back.

Figure 4. Example of a prose layout.
(Published in *The Writer's Voice* and read on BBC Radio Merseyside)

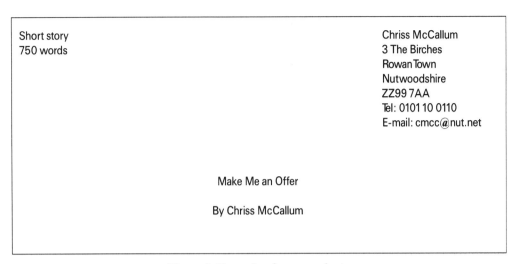

Figure 5. Example of a cover sheet.

The final check

Before you pack up your work for posting, give it a final read through. Reprint any pages where you've marked corrections.

Pen names

If you want to use a pen name, type it in the byline under the title, but *not* above your address.

DEALING WITH ILLUSTRATIONS

If you're writing articles, good photographs can help sell your work. In fact, some magazines won't consider articles without them. Your ability to take quality photos will greatly enhance your value as a freelance article writer. Take a course, if you need to. Most editors welcome a 'words-and-pictures' package.

Check what kind of photos your target publication (or book publisher) prefers. Most publications now use digital technology, but it's best to check.

If your subject requires diagrams, maps, line drawings and the like, it's usually acceptable to send roughs for the staff artist to work from. If you can supply the artwork to a professional standard yourself, send photocopies.

Don't stick illustrations onto the ms. Pencil *very lightly* an identification number on the back of each one, and pencil the corresponding numbers at appropriate places in the ms margins. Page layouts might not allow illustrations to go exactly where you want them, but they'll be placed as near as possible. Type the captions on a separate sheet and number them to correspond with the illustrations.

TIP

Photographs can double your chances of acceptance.

SELECTING AND STUDYING A SUITABLE MARKET

For novels and non-fiction books, see the relevant chapters.

To sell to magazines or newspapers, you need to have a clear idea of your target market *before* you begin to write your article or story. Too many new writers – and some others who should know better – write the piece, revise it, polish it up, *then* start looking for an outlet.

Successful writers don't work that way. They write with a specific market in mind, a market they've already studied in detail. They tailor the content, treatment, style and length of the work to suit that market. As a beginning writer, you must do the same, so that you can compete at a professional level.

Market study is just common sense

There's no great mystique about it. Think of your writing as a product you're making for sale. No, don't frown and say you couldn't possibly think about creative writing in that way. If you're serious about selling your work, you *must* think like that. You're entering into a business transaction, little different from selling birdseed or a three-piece suite. You are the manufacturer, and you have to supply what the retailer wants. An editor is a retailer. He buys from the manufacturer – the writer – what he knows he can sell to his customers – his readers.

— WISE WORDS—

The fiction editor of *Woman's Weekly* won't buy a horror story. She knows she would lose readers if she did. Mills & Boon won't buy a political novel. A literary magazine would have no slot for a DIY article. Only the postal service benefits from misdirected submissions like these.

At the very least, make sure your work is targeted at the right area of publishing, an area that uses *that kind of material.*

Start by studying the *latest* editions of the *Writers' & Artists' Yearbook* and *The Writer's Handbook*. Read right through the appropriate sections. Don't just look up the names you already know. There might be other potential markets you don't know about.

Select the most appropriate outlets and take a close analytical look to see what prospects they hold for you, as a new freelance writer. Buy copies or read them on the Internet if they're available online, and send for guidelines.

— WISE WORDS—

Train yourself to shoot with a rifle – not with a scattergun.

Later in the book you'll find sources of information about markets in the various fields. For the moment, let's look at the general principles of market study:

1. *Before you send anything*, check that the market you have in mind will consider submissions from freelance writers.

2. Make sure the treatment and style of your work is suitable for your target market.

3. Check that the length of the work suits the publisher's stated word limits.

Let's look at these three points in detail, because if you get any of them wrong you could damage your credibility as well as losing a sale. Careless marketing warns an editor that you're not taking your business seriously.

Are freelance offerings welcome?

Start with the publication itself. Look at the masthead, the column listing the names of the editor and other staff. There might be a notice, possibly in tiny print, stating something like 'No responsibility taken for unsolicited mss' (indicating that submissions will at least be read) or 'No unsolicited mss' (meaning that they won't be considered under any circumstances). If there's no information in the masthead, look through the whole publication – the notice might be tucked away somewhere.

The *Writers' & Artists' Yearbook* can usually guide you on whether unsolicited material is welcome or not. Writers' magazines carry current editorial 'wants', and most check them at source.

Check the publication's website. You can often find detailed information there on how they like to be approached.

If you can't find specific information anywhere, phone or (preferably) e-mail the editorial office and ask.

Don't ask for free sample copies. If it's a trade or professional publication or any other that you can't find in the shops, ask if they'll send you a copy or two *with an invoice*. If they invoice you, pay up.

> **— WISE WORDS—**
>
> Your market study is your responsibility. It's neither reasonable nor professional to ask another business to subsidise yours.

You can get quicker answers to your questions, of course, if you ring the editorial office. Most don't mind this, as long as you keep your conversation brief and to the point. Ask for the editorial office at a magazine, or the appropriate department at a publishing house.

Prepare a short list of questions before you phone, so you get *all* the answers you need. You might want to ask, for example:

1. Do you welcome unsolicited material from freelance writers?
2. Are any subjects covered exclusively by your staff?
3. What lengths do you prefer?
4. Do you like a query first, or would you rather see the whole piece?
5. Do you have guidelines I could send for?

Add any other questions pertinent to a particular market. For example, if the answer to Question 1 is 'Yes' and you already know what you want to offer, ask for the name of the appropriate editor so you can address your offering to a specific name.

Don't go into detail about what you're writing unless they ask you. Be as brief and businesslike as you can. All you need at this stage is basic information.

TIP

Always address your query or submission to a particular person by name. This gets your envelope straight onto someone's desk rather than onto an anonymous pile.

Is your material suitable?

Submit *only* appropriate material. As a beginner, you would be wise to stick to familiar ground and write for publications you already know and like. Wait till you have some experience before you try to widen your scope. You know why *you* buy your favourite publications, you're familiar with their content, so you won't send them something you wouldn't expect to find there yourself.

Get the tone and style right

Collect several *recent* copies of your target publication. It can be worse than useless to study copies from months or even weeks ago, because editorial policies change frequently. See Chapter 7 for detailed advice on analysing magazines.

Get the length right

Most of the markets listed in the yearbooks specify a minimum and/or maximum number of words for submissions. There's no point in ignoring these stipulated word limits. Editors have a certain amount of space to fill, and they won't alter either their policy or the size of their publication to accommodate a 3,000-word story if their stated limit is 2,000 words. Nor will a 50,000-word novel find a place in a list that only publishes 200,000-word blockbusters.

Keep up to date

You're stepping into a business that never stands still. Magazines vanish, new ones appear. Big publishers eat up little ones. Rebels set up on their own. Editors move about and take their policies and their favourite writers with them.

Don't rely on last year's reference books. You could waste far more money on misdirected mss than it would cost to update them. Use the Internet to confirm that your research is totally up to date – it's a wonderful resource for writers.

Before you send off *any* submission, or even a query letter, check that:

◆ Your target market is willing to consider it.
◆ What you're sending or enquiring about is suitable for that market.
◆ You've written your material in an appropriate style.
◆ You've complied with the stipulated word limits.
◆ Your market research is bang up to date.

HOW AGENTS WORK

Mention agents at any writers' gathering and you can expect heated argument all round. The most common complaint heard from unpublished or little-published writers is that 'agents don't want to know you till you've already made it'.

This might be true in some cases, but it's far more likely that these disappointed writers' work has been rejected by agents for the same reason that most mss are rejected by publishers and editors. Simply, they are not good enough to publish. An agent won't take on the job of trying to place a manuscript in which he has no confidence, any more than a publisher will accept a book he knows he won't be able to sell.

Note
Very few agents handle short stories or articles except, perhaps, from established book authors already on their lists.

A good agent chooses his clients very carefully because he'll be committing himself to a lot of work on their behalf. This caution is understandable – the agent makes no money till his author does, and what he eventually makes will be a percentage of what that author's book earns. Contrary to what some writers believe, most agents work hard for their money.

If an agent does take you on, he'll want to establish a mutually profitable partnership with you. Your agent will secure better terms from publishers, and will know the home *and* overseas markets well enough to exploit the rights in your book as fully as possible. Yes, he gets 10 or 15 per cent of the profits – but *you* get 85 or 90 per cent, and that could well be a healthy percentage of sales you wouldn't have got without the agent.

Try to get an agent straight away if you want to, but be realistic. Your chances of a favourable response are about the same as your chances of acceptance by a publisher. Neither will want a substandard piece of work.

The *Writers' & Artists' Yearbook* and *The Writer's Handbook* both list agents, with information on what they handle and what they don't. Choose one with an interest in the kind of work you're producing, otherwise you'll have no chance at all. Most of the listed agents specify their preferred method of approach – you won't impress them if you don't respect this.

Now you should know:

◆ How to prepare a prose manuscript.
◆ How to deal with illustrations.
◆ How to select and study a suitable market.
◆ How agents work.

6

Submitting Your Work to the Market

You only get one chance to make a first impression. Make sure it's a good one.

In this chapter:

- approaching the market
- following up your submission
- coping with rejection.

APPROACHING THE MARKET

Every detail of your approach should give a positive impression of your professionalism. Here's how to do that:

1. Whatever you're sending, enclose a covering letter. You want to establish contact with the editor, and your covering letter acts as an introductory handshake. Covering letters and letters of enquiry should be typed as normal business letters, single spaced, *not* double spaced like manuscripts.

2. Keep your letter brief and to the point. You'll find examples in the appropriate chapters. (A letter of enquiry sent by itself, of course, needs more detail.)

3. Find out the name of the appropriate editor. Look in the masthead, check the website or ring the switchboard and ask for the name you need. *Don't* address anything 'To whom it may concern' or 'Dear sir/madam' or anything like that.

4. Enclose an SAE big enough and bearing adequate postage for the return of your work, otherwise you may never see your ms again. Every publishing office has at least one drawer full of unsolicited mss that can't be returned.

The editor didn't invite them, so why should he pay for returning them? Small Press magazines in particular can't afford this expense.

5. If you're sending an ms that's disposable if it isn't wanted, tell the editor so, and enclose a business-size SAE so he can let you know his decision – otherwise you won't know whether you can send it out again or not.

6. If you want to be sure your ms arrived safely, enclose a stamped self-addressed postcard on which you've written the title of the work and the name of the market you're sending it to.

And how not to ...

1. Don't tell the editor the story of your life, your writing career, and how much your family, friends and writers' circle admire your work.

2. Don't embarrass the editor with emotional blackmail. His heart will sink and his hackles will rise if you tell him you need the money to feed your children, or you're 99 and might not survive beyond his next issue, or your doctor has prescribed creative writing as therapy after your breakdown and a rejection could tip you over the edge again. (Yes, people do these things.)

3. Don't be grovelling, condescending or demanding – just be businesslike. Any other approach will cast doubts on your professionalism and could suggest you might be less than a joy to work with.

4. Don't send anything to more than one magazine at a time – editors don't like this. (You *can* send the same book proposal to more than one publisher or agent at the same time. This is accepted practice now.)

5. Don't use umpteen-times recycled envelopes. We all like to save trees – and money – but keep economy labels and sticky tape for your private letters. In business, such economies are counter-productive. They project entirely the wrong image, that of the amateur 'scribbler'. And don't send an SAE that makes the editor cringe and wonder how often it's been licked already. Don't use your day-job company's headed paper, or send your ms in an envelope bearing the company's logo and franked at its expense. This has the taint of petty stinginess, and does not inspire confidence.

RED LIGHT

William Brohaugh, former editor of *Writer's Digest* magazine, says in his book *Professional Etiquette for Writers* that using recycled envelopes to present your work is 'like wearing a crumpled suit to a job interview'.

Checklist

Before you send anything out, check the following:

1. You are contacting an appropriate market.

2. You are following that market's preferred method of approach.

3. You are sending it to the appropriate editor.

4. Your covering letter/letter of enquiry is businesslike and to the point.

5. You've enclosed a suitable SAE with your story or article, or enough return postage with your full-length ms.

6. Your stationery is crisp and clean, as is appropriate to your professionalism.

RED LIGHT

Phrase your letter with discretion, weighing the effect your words will have on the editor who reads them. For instance, the following sentences are guaranteed to trigger editorial alarm:

- 'Here is a short story that is a good deal better than those you've been publishing lately.'
- 'Rejection won't discourage me. It's my life's ambition to get published in your magazine, and I'll keep trying till I do.'
- 'You will appreciate that I am a beginner, which is why I'm sending my work to you before I try to get published in something more literary ...'
- 'Caution: this story is copyright and I have taken the precaution of lodging a dated copy with my solicitor ...'

FOLLOWING UP YOUR SUBMISSION

If you don't get a response in, say, three months, enquire about the status of your ms, either by e-mail, letter or telephone. If this gets no response either, you'll have to decide whether to try another outlet or wait a bit longer. Most magazines and publishing houses have cut staff to the bone so there's usually a backlog.

However, courtesy should work both ways. If you feel you're being dealt with unfairly, advise the editor *in writing* that the ms you sent is no longer on offer. Keep a copy of the letter. (You did keep a copy of the work, didn't you?)

RED LIGHT
Never send out your only copy of any piece of work.

COPING WITH REJECTION

Rejection – a dismal word for a depressing event: an editor has refused your brain-child. It happens to (almost) every writer. Hardly surprising, with dozens of submissions battling for every opening.

The best coping strategy is to build up a regular output. Always have work in hand as well as out on offer. Don't invest all your dreams in one ms.

And if your ms does thud back onto your doormat, please don't:

- Tear it up and throw it away.
- Iron it and send it straight out again.
- Write an indignant letter to the editor, questioning his decision, his brains and his ancestry.
- Spread jam on the rejection slip and send it back.

Instead, try to analyse what went wrong. Start developing your ability to criticise your own work objectively. Answer the questions in the following checklist. Be honest – if you refuse to face the truth you're only fooling yourself.

Checklist

1. Are you sure the work is as good *in every way* as you could possibly make it?

2. Did you check every fact and reference?

3. Are you sure you sent the work to a suitable market?

4. Did you check *for yourself* that your target market is currently open to unsolicited mss?

5. Did you check *for yourself* that the slot you aimed at is not usually or exclusively written by staff or by commissioned writers?

6. Did you analyse your market thoroughly?

7. Did you tailor the style, tone, language and length to your market's requirements?

8. Did you check your spelling, grammar, punctuation and syntax?

9. Did you show an accurate word count?

10. Did you present an ms that is clean, clear, neat, typed on plain white A4 paper, double spaced, on one side of the paper only, with decent margins?

If you answered 'no' or 'not sure' to any of these questions, your approach has been less than totally professional. It doesn't pay to skimp on the hard work.

What if your answers are all 'yes'? Then perhaps your work was rejected because:

◆ However wonderful you, your best friend or your writers' group believe it to be, the work does not meet publishable standards. Maybe you didn't research, organise or write it well enough – or maybe it's just plain dull. Sorry to be blunt, but these are the reasons for most rejections.

◆ The publisher already has a stock of this kind of material. Yours would have to be sensational to be bought at this time. You're out of luck with your timing – a hazard of freelancing.

- The editor has recently bought/commissioned/published something similar. The first two are simple misfortunes. The third could indicate less than thorough market research.

- The editor didn't like what you sent him. If he doesn't bother to tell you this, you'll never know. Another editor might love it.

— WISE WORDS —

When an editor turns down your work he is making a business decision. There is nothing personal involved.

Two questions new writers often ask:

Do editors really read every submission they receive?
The answer to that is 'yes'. And 'no'. Yes, they do look at everything that comes in – no one would consciously risk missing a gem. But no, they don't read every ms all the way through. They don't need to. A rapid scan tells an experienced editor whether a submission, be it a query or a complete ms, is of potential value _to him_. If he doesn't think it is, he won't waste time on it.

It's pointless to try to catch out a 'lazy' or 'prejudiced' editor. So forget the hair or the spot of glue between the pages. They prove nothing.

Why don't editors tell me where I'm going wrong?
Few editors offer advice to writers. Some writers, especially beginners, think this is unfair. However, there are good reasons:

- Lack of time. With 100-plus mss arriving every week, even a few minutes spent giving advice on each one would occupy hours of an editor's working day – and it isn't his job anyway.

- As explained above, the editor doesn't need to read the whole ms to know if it interests him or not, and advice based on less than a thorough critical reading can be worse than no advice at all.

◆ An editor is employed to fill his publication with suitable material, *not* to give writing tutorials. The writing is *your* job. If you send something that's almost right, the editor *might* give you some pointers and ask for a rewrite 'on spec'. Remember, though, that you're offering work for sale in a commercial marketplace. If you were selling lampshades, you wouldn't ask your customers to show you how to make them, would you?

RED LIGHT
Don't interpret a few kind words as an invitation to rewrite and re-submit. Do this *only* if you're specifically invited to.

How books are dealt with

Most publishers employ freelance readers to read and report on book manuscripts. These are usually experienced editors, authors and academics, and it's on their recommendation that an ms is either rejected outright or passed on to a second reader or an in-house editor.

A publisher's reader has no authority to accept a book, but his decision that one should be rejected is seldom questioned. Acceptance rates for unsolicited book mss are low. One publisher's reader told me he has only seen two out of the 5,000 or so books he's assessed actually get into print. (This is not the glamorous job many people think it is.)

Do keep a sense of proportion, then, if the first publisher on your list rejects your first novel. You are certainly not alone.

DID YOU KNOW?
M*A*S*H was rejected by 21 publishers. Enid Blyton collected 500 rejections. Crime writer John Creasey, author of 564 published books, received 774 rejections before selling his first story. Dr Seuss's first children's book was rejected by 27 publishers. John Grisham's first novel, *A Time to Kill*, was rejected by 15 publishers and 30 agents.

If you must let off steam ...

If it makes you feel better, write a venomous letter – *but don't post it*. Such a response would not be forgotten or forgiven.

The following 'rejections of rejections' are not recommended either:

- 'Please read this again. I feel sure you must have missed the whole point of the story ...'

- 'It was with considerable amazement that I received my returned manuscript this morning. I would have thought that the least you could do was to tell me what you thought was wrong with it. Here is another story. Kindly let me have a swift response, with your reasons in full should you reject this one ...'

- 'How could you! Your rejection has cut me to the quick! I may never have the confidence to write another word ...'

- 'You don't have the guts to give an original talent a chance ...'

- 'I am returning your rejection slip herewith. I regret it is not suited to my requirements at present ...'

Recommended reading

Jack Canfield, Mark Victor Hansen and Bud Gardner (eds), *Chicken Soup for the Writer's Soul*.
Barnaby Conrad and Monte Schulz, *Snoopy's Guide to the Writing Life*.
Rachael Stock, *The Insider's Guide to Getting Your Book Published*.

Now you should know:

- How to market your work effectively.
- How to follow up your submission without alienating the editor.
- How to deal positively with rejection.

7

Writing for Magazines and Newspapers

Take a look around any major newsagent's shelves. Did you realise that nearly all the publications you see there buy most of their material from freelance writers? Writing factual material for magazines and newspapers offers a fast and potentially lucrative route to publication. The constant demand for good articles makes them the easiest type of writing to sell. However, easy to sell does not mean easy to write. The demand is high, but the standard expected is also high.

In this chapter:

♦ what it takes to write successful articles
♦ finding markets
♦ article types
♦ analysing a magazine
♦ choosing your topic
♦ writing a saleable article
♦ writing seasonal and anniversary material
♦ selling your article
♦ looking at journalism
♦ photography for article writers
♦ writing for overseas magazines.

WHAT IT TAKES TO WRITE SUCCESSFUL ARTICLES

Every writer – and that includes you – has knowledge and experience that could interest, help, enrich or simply entertain other people. There are publications about every imaginable subject from architecture to zoology, with openings for all types of writing from readers' letters to in-depth features.

To write for magazines, you need:

♦ The ability to write clear, concise English.
♦ An observant eye.
♦ An enquiring mind.
♦ A professional attitude to writing and selling your material.

TIP
A portfolio of published articles will open the door to professional writers' organisations.

FINDING MARKETS

There are literally thousands of potential outlets for articles. The *Writers' & Artists' Yearbook* lists more than 600 UK newspapers and magazines that publish and pay for articles. *Willing's Press Guide* (expensive – ask at the reference library) lists more than 10,000 UK publications, including trade, professional and specialist magazines. Many of these welcome freelance contributions relevant to their subject areas.

Writers' News (and its sister publication *Writing Magazine*, which you can find in newsagents), *Writer's Forum* and *The New Writer* also carry market news. The Bureau of Freelance Photographers' *Market Newsletter* has market information for photo-journalists.

ARTICLE TYPES

Magazines and newspapers use articles of every imaginable type. Look at the choice:

♦ Readers' letters, fillers and mini-articles.
♦ Interviews.
♦ Personality profiles.
♦ Personal experience.
♦ Human interest and 'real-life' stories.
♦ Anniversary articles.

- Seasonal articles.
- Opinion pieces.
- Historical articles.
- Nostalgia pieces.
- Travel pieces.
- 'How-to' and 'DIY'.
- Self-help and self-improvement.

ANALYSING A MAGAZINE

To succeed in today's markets, you need to understand your target publication's ethos, style and readership.

General readers look at a magazine in a casual way. They notice the cover, glance at the contents list, read the sections that interest them and maybe flick through the rest. As an aspiring contributor, however, you must take a much closer and more analytical view. You need to build a picture in your mind of the publication's target readership to be able to understand what the editors and writers are aiming to do.

Get writers' guidelines if they are available and read them carefully. (Check the reference books, consult the website or ring the editorial office and ask.) Don't rely on guidelines alone, though. Successful market study needs a 'hands-on' approach.

Take a notepad and analyse your target magazine as follows.

The cover
- What does the cover picture tell you about the magazine?

- What does the text on the cover tell you about the type of reader likely to be attracted to this particular publication?

The list of contents
- What subjects are the main features about?

◆ What are the regular 'departments' and columns about? If there is a list of staff names, check these against the bylines – these sections might not be open to freelance contributions.

◆ What type of article does the magazine appear to favour?

◆ What do the article titles tell you about the writing tone?

The editor's message

Most magazine editors write a comment column at or near the beginning of the magazine, a 'Welcome to my magazine' message. Read this closely.

◆ What subjects does the editor talk about?

◆ What do these comments tell you about the magazine's attitude and/or ethos?

◆ What kind of writing style does the editor use?

The readership

◆ Who would the publication appeal to most? Men? Women? Both sexes? A specialist readership? Or a general readership?

◆ In what age group?

◆ What do the advertisements tell you? Advertisers spend their money shrewdly – on ads in the publications most likely to be read by people to whom their products will appeal. Stair lifts and walk-in baths indicate an older age group than sports equipment and family holidays. Catalogue clothing suggests a less affluent readership than department-store fashion. Ads give you a true 'feel' for the readership in terms of age, lifestyle, disposable income, education, interests and hobbies.

The readers' letters

◆ What do these tell you about the typical reader's attitudes to life, likes and dislikes, interests, social concerns, family concerns and so on?

If there are short stories

◆ What do they tell you about the type of reader the magazine aims to attract?

◆ How many are published in a typical issue?

◆ How does this compare to the number of articles? (See Chapter 8 for detailed advice on writing and marketing short stories.)

The articles

◆ Do they cover a range of topics, or are they narrowly focused?

◆ Are they written in similar styles? A variety of styles?

◆ How would you describe the overall tone of the writing?

◆ What kind of leads (introductory paragraphs) do they have?

◆ What type of endings do they have?

◆ Look at the language used. Are the sentences long or short? Simple and straightforward? Or long and complex? Are the words short and everyday? Or multi-syllable and 'Help – where's the dictionary!'?

◆ Are most of the paragraphs short and sharp? Or long and dense?

◆ Are photographs included? Sidebars? Graphics? Tables? Other illustrative elements?

◆ Are the writers named? Are any/most of these names well known? Do any of them appear on the list of the publication's staff?

CHOOSING YOUR TOPIC

As a beginner, you could try fillers or readers' letters to start with. A filler is a short item fitted into a small space so that a page won't be left with blank paper where the main items don't quite fill it.

Anecdotes, humorous verse, puzzles, jokes, cartoons, tips and hints, press errors, odd facts, brain-teasers, quotations – all these are used as fillers, and many magazines buy them from freelances.

Keep an eye open for likely filler slots, and collect odd pieces of information, jokes, 'overheards', amazing facts and suchlike.

Readers' letters have acquired a status of their own and are now a strong selling feature for many publications. Payment can be as high as £50-plus, though the average is £5–£25 (more when photographs are included) and some magazines 'pay' in prizes rather than cash.

The 'Readers' Letters' slot provides a starting point for many new writers. This section might be headed something like 'Letters to the Editor', 'Your letters', 'You say ...' or the like. These letters are usually quite short, but 'short' doesn't equal 'easy'. A successful letter has probably been crafted to the needs of its market as carefully as an article.

> ### — WISE WORDS —
>
> Readers' letters are good practice for an aspiring article writer because they demand the same kind of disciplines: no waffle, no wordiness, and they must make their point as clearly and concisely as possible.

Points to note
◆ Are most of the published letters long or short?

◆ Is their general tone neutral? Passionate? Cosy? Argumentative? Cynical? Amused? Helpful? Sympathetic?

◆ How many are obvious responses to correspondence or features in previous issues?

Don't bother sending an SAE, unless you're enclosing photographs you want returned. Letters are seldom acknowledged, and no voucher copies are sent. You *might* get advance notice of publication, or you might hear nothing at all till you receive your payment.

Recommended reading
Alison Chisholm, *How to Write Five Minute Features*, which includes tips on writing readers' letters.

Chriss McCallum, *Writing How-To Articles and Books*, which includes a section on fillers and tips.

When you're ready to move on

The usual advice given to beginners is to write about what you know. That's sound counsel up to a point, but don't let it put you off tackling a subject you know little about but would like to explore. My advice is to write about what interests and inspires you, and to back up your enthusiasm with any necessary research. If you *care* about your subject enough, your reader will know – and your first reader will be an editor.

Maybe you're already familiar with publications you believe might welcome your contribution. Could you write more than one article on your subject, slanting each to a different market?

For example, if your hobby is collecting old musical recordings, you could write about:

- where to find them
- how much they cost
- how to store them
- equipment to play them
- the artists who made them

... and much, much more, as the subject diagram in Figure 6 shows.

Try making your own subject diagram in the same way. This kind of lateral thinking, sometimes called 'clustering' or 'mind-mapping', is a lot more productive than making linear lists. It's a powerful brainstormer. Try using different coloured pens for this exercise – they introduce an element of playfulness and help your brain to relax.

You can also use this exercise to map out information sources and possible markets. Ideas will flow as fast as you can write them down.

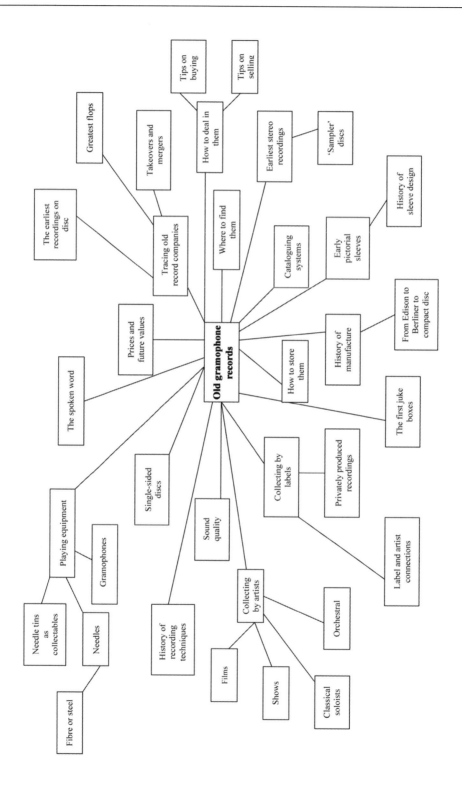

Figure 6. Example of a subject diagram.

WRITING A SALEABLE ARTICLE

Whatever your subject, your article should be structured in a logical and satisfying form. Like a good story, it needs a beginning, a middle and an end, in a straightforward sequence (unlike fiction, where you can take liberties with the order of things):

1. Begin with a strong opening paragraph. If you've dug up some interesting or little-known fact, or if you have a strong statement to make, put it here. Beginners often save their juiciest fact till the end, aiming to end with a bang. But if you don't grab and hold your reader's interest right away (and remember that your first reader will be your target editor, possibly at the end of a long day) he might not bother to read to the end, so your amazing revelation is wasted. Feed your reader your tastiest titbit first, and save the second-best to last.

   Here's an example of an opening paragraph:

   'For all her success, queen of crime-writers Agatha Christie was a frustrated author. Her world-famous detective creations, Miss Marple and Hercule Poirot, made her rich and famous, but they were "work" and gave her only a fraction of the satisfaction she found in writing her "Mary Westmacott" novels.'

2. The middle section should be packed with interesting information written in the most logical sequence, but not presented simply as a list of facts. Spice it with anecdotes, questions, opinions.

3. The closing paragraph should provide a satisfying rounding-off, summarising in some way what you've been saying. It can be very effective to refer back, however obliquely, to your first paragraph.

   And an example of a closing paragraph:

   'In her autobiography, Agatha Christie described Hercule Poirot as an albatross hanging round her neck. Writers beware – make sure the series character you're working so hard to create is one you love enough to live with happily for years to come.'

Make it convincing

It's essential that you gather enough information and solid facts, and give enough thought to your subject, to write a convincing, fact-packed article that reflects your own views. The editorial nose will soon sniff out a 'scissors-and-paste' job – that is, a piece cobbled together from reference books and other people's opinions. Of course, you can make use of other writers' findings and conclusions (provided you don't plagiarise their words) but your article will be stillborn if it isn't enriched by your own thoughts and feelings.

You might find it takes several rewrites to achieve a convincingly 'spontaneous' style, but don't rewrite the life out of it, and don't be afraid to let your own personality shine through.

Be methodical

You'll save yourself much time and trouble if you devise a simple system for filing your information as you gather it. It's infuriating if you're stuck for one small piece of information and can't remember where you stored it.

You need to be able to retrieve everything quickly and easily. This is especially important if your writing time is limited, maybe sandwiched between your day job and keeping the weeds down.

You can use document wallets, large envelopes, card index systems or, of course, electronic storage on your computer (don't forget to back everything up). It doesn't matter what system you use – it does matter that you have one.

WRITING SEASONAL AND ANNIVERSARY MATERIAL

'Seasonal material' is writing related to a particular season of the year: Christmas, Easter, Valentine's Day, Mother's Day, New Year and so on.

Seasonal material must be submitted well in advance, anything from four months to a year or even more. It's no use offering a Christmas story in October – the Christmas issue will be on its way to the shops by then.

Check your target publication's seasonal deadlines. If the guidelines don't tell you, phone the editorial department and ask. No one will mind, as long as you keep your call brief and businesslike.

TIP
Write your seasonal pieces *during the season*. It's hard, for example, to get into a 'mistletoe-and-holly' mood when you're drooping over a hot keyboard on a sweltering summer's day. File the piece away, noting the appropriate submission date in your diary. Get your ms out a few days early and read it objectively. You might see faults you missed, and this gives you time to correct them and to give the work the final polish that can make the difference between a sale and a rejection.

'Anniversary material' deals with past events and is intended for publication on or near an anniversary of those events. Like seasonal material, anniversary pieces must be submitted well in advance.

As a beginner, you would probably be wasting your time if you wrote about an event like, for example, D-Day or a Royal wedding, unless you've unearthed something new and/or sensational. You could try sending a query, but most editors will already have material on the subject either in stock or commissioned from regular contributors or from famous 'names'.

Local papers and magazines might welcome features about the anniversaries of interesting local people and events, especially if you can link them to something that's happening today. With local knowledge, you could produce a feature packed with facts and human interest – and that's the kind that sells.

— WISE WORDS —
Don't refer to current events unless your piece is intended for the current year only. The magazine won't want to hold it on file for future use.

SELLING YOUR ARTICLE

It's usual nowadays to send a query, either by letter or by e-mail, before you submit an article. This has long been the practice in the US, and most American editors insist on it. Unsolicited material is firmly discouraged.

In the UK, though, it's usually acceptable to send in a very short article of 500 words or so without a preliminary query – the query would take almost as long to read as the article. You won't get a firm acceptance on the strength of a query anyway, so you might as well let the editor see what you can do. If he prefers a query, he'll let you know.

For anything longer, send a query first. The editor might ask you to take a different angle, or write to a shorter or longer length than you suggested.

Writing a query letter

Your query letter should tell the editor:

1. Your subject, and the angle you plan to take. Use bullets to list your points briefly and clearly, and indicate the proposed wordage.

2. Why you think his readers would be interested in what you have to say.

3. Why you are the right person to write this piece. If you have special qualifications – practical experience, a degree in the subject, for instance – include them here, but don't drag in irrelevancies. For example, if you're offering an article on Commonwealth memorial stamps, your 20-year devotion to yoga won't impress.

Suppose you want to offer a general interest magazine an article on collecting ephemera, those throwaway bits of social history: postcards, programmes, tickets, bookmarks and the like. First, check that you have the *current* editor's name, *correctly spelled*. Then structure your query on the lines of the letter in Figure 7.

Emily Hoarder
White Elephants
Overflow Lane
Fillingham XX5 5XX
Tel: 01 001 0001
E-mail: EmilyH@XYZ.com

10th October 200X

David Payer
Editor
Take Anything Magazine
Anytown S1 1XX

Dear Mr Payer

Would you be interested in an article on collecting ephemera? There is great scope in this field for building an interesting and potentially valuable collection, without too great a financial outlay. Many of your readers might not know how collectable these scraps of social history have now become. Some might not know that such a field of collecting exists.

To begin a collection, they would need to know:

♦   what the term 'ephemera' means: items of no intrinsic value, such as postcards, cigarette cards, bookmarks, tickets, magazines and newspapers, advertising material, pamphlets and so on;
♦   where to look for collectable items: antique and collectors' fairs, jumble sales, charity shops, car boot sales, the attics and cellars of friends and relatives ...
♦   approximate prices they might expect to pay;
♦   where the greatest potential lies for increases in value;
♦   how to store and/or display their collection.

Once a new collector realises how wide the range is, he or she often moves on to specialisation, and is soon hooked on the hobby. It's fun, it's fascinating and it's affordable.

I have been collecting ephemera myself for several years, and have recently begun to specialise in bookmarks, their history and design, and their value to the companies that issued them (they were widely used as an advertising medium).

The text as I plan it would be 1,750–2,000 words, and I can supply a variety of photographs, old and new.

I enclose a stamped addressed envelope, and look forward to hearing from you.

Yours sincerely

Emily Hoarder

Figure 7. Writing a query letter.

LOOKING AT JOURNALISM

A successful journalist is a writer who knows how to:

- Tell his story with a precise focus.
- See his story from his reader's angle.
- Avoid verbosity.
- Cut out padding.
- Express his meaning in clear, concise, unambiguous language.
- Produce quality work under pressure to meet tight deadlines.

Most newspapers, like most magazines, buy material from freelance writers. There are three main types of newspaper: national, regional and local. The *Writers' & Artists' Yearbook* lists all the nationals and a few of the larger regionals, but *The Writer's Handbook* gives more information in this field, listing all the major national and regional titles, with editorial names and requirements, tips on approaching them, and what they pay.

RED LIGHT

It's a mistake to rely on reference books for staff names – they could be out of date even before the book is published. Check them yourself.

The financial rewards

Payment varies a great deal. Some papers pay NUJ (National Union of Journalists) rates whether you're a member or not. Others pay 'by arrangement', meaning you'll be offered what the editor thinks the piece is worth – or possibly, if he's never heard of you, what he thinks you'll be prepared to settle for. A thoroughly professional approach can pay off here. Don't encourage the editor to offer you a pittance because your careless presentation and your tatty envelopes tell him you know nothing and care even less about the business.

Unless you're already a member of the NUJ, there's no point in challenging the offer. Either refuse it and try your luck elsewhere, or accept it philosophically so you can add another item to your tally of published work. A strong portfolio will eventually put you in a position to negotiate fees, as more and more publications are asking for clips to be included with queries.

TIP

Each edition of *The Writer's Handbook* gives current NUJ payment rates for national and provincial newspapers and for magazines.

Getting your foot in the door

You could try local papers. They always want:

- News stories, short and to the point, covering local items: 'Her Majesty unveils memorial plaque', 'Local grandmother's surprise triplets'.

- Social issues articles: 'Save our swimming baths!', 'Do our citizens want clean streets?'

- Striking photographs of local people, places and events.

TIP

'Local' means keeping the focus on the area. For example, 'Main street grocer lost at sea' was a headline referring to a man who went down with the *Titanic*.

If you spot an opening for a topic your paper isn't already covering, you could suggest ideas, perhaps for:

- A book, film, TV or DVD column.
- A poetry corner.
- A children's page.
- An original series that *you* could supply on a regular basis.

Don't suggest any kind of competition, though, unless you're willing to handle the entries yourself. The staff won't welcome the extra work.

The five 'W's

When you're writing your article, make sure you include all essential information. Check the content against the journalist's creed, the five 'W's:

◆ Who?
◆ What?
◆ Where?
◆ When?
◆ Why?

And if it's appropriate, add an 'H' for 'How?'

Whether distributed free or not, these papers live on their advertising revenue, so short pieces stand a better chance because they leave more room for ads.

Include a photo or two if you can. Check with the paper about preferred formats.

Check deadlines, too – this week's hot news is next week's rejection.

You'll usually be paid after publication, at some set date, and you might be expected to submit an invoice. Clarify this beforehand. An invoice is a simple business document, a bill asking for payment of money due to you. It's easy to prepare. Make sure you include all the necessary information, as in Figure 8.

PHOTOGRAPHY FOR ARTICLE WRITERS

You'll increase your chances of success many times over if you can supply interesting photographs to supplement your articles.

When you're researching your market, note what proportion of photographs to text your target publication uses, what proportion of colour to black and white, then check with the editor:

◆ Whether they use photos supplied by the writer – some publications prefer to use staff photographers or library photos.

INVOICE

Oliver Columnist
12 Gossip Alley
Tiny Tiles
Eastborough X12 21X
E-mail: OllyC@XY.net

22nd July 200X

Basil Bond
Editor
Eastborough Tattle
Eastborough A22 22X

To supplying one short feature: 'Scandal at the Vicarage'
Plus 3 b/w photographs
Published in Eastborough Tattle 15/07/0X   £35.00

Figure 8. Example of an invoice.

◆ If they want photos from you, how they like these to be supplied – as prints or as electronic files, and if the latter, what format they prefer.

TIP

Most publications accept digital images, but check what quality and format they require.

Consider subscribing to the Bureau of Freelance Photographers, where you can get technical advice and market information specially gathered for photographers and photo-journalists. (See under Associations Open to Unpublished Writers at the end of the book.)

WRITING FOR OVERSEAS MAGAZINES

The whole English-speaking world is open to you, and it's huge.

The *Writers' & Artists' Yearbook* lists a selection of magazines and newspapers in Australia, Canada, New Zealand and South Africa. For the USA, the *Yearbook* gives information on book publishers and literary agents but does not list specific magazines or newspapers, referring readers to other sources of information. It does give advice on submitting material to the USA, though. We'll look at the North American market in more detail below.

The Writer's Handbook has substantial sections on US book publishers and literary agents, plus US contacts based in the UK.

The Internet has more information than you could ever use on overseas magazines and newspapers. Ask your favourite search engine to find, for example, 'North American magazines' and you'll be offered lists that it would take weeks just to read. Explore any country's publications in this way, and take your pick. Most magazines post guidelines on their websites, and many let you read current or past issues on-screen.

TIP
Look at other countries where there are large numbers of English speakers – India, for example.

Rights

You can offer material already published in the UK to overseas magazines *provided you've only sold British rights.*

Although both publications cover copyright law, the *Writers' & Artists' Yearbook* and *The Writer's Handbook* give no guidance on rights bought by specific magazines. The American *Writer's Market* (see below) does give this information for specific magazines.

Writing for North American magazines

The most comprehensive guide to North American markets is *Writer's Market*, published annually by Writer's Digest Books, Cincinnati. (*Note*: Don't confuse this guide with the recently launched UK *Writer's Market* from publishers David & Charles.) With 1,000-plus pages in every edition, *Writer's Market* is packed with markets for every kind of writing, giving details of pay rates, royalties, advances, specific editorial needs and submission guidelines. You can order it through major bookshops, buy it from Amazon.co.uk, or subscribe to the online version at www.writersmarket.com.

Most American magazines ask for 'North American Rights'. These rights usually cover Canada, too, so you can't offer the same piece to both a US and a Canadian market.

Nearly all US magazines issue comprehensive writers' guidelines. They find this saves time and trouble for their staff as well as for potential contributors. With Internet access, you can look them up on the websites. Alternatively, you can request guidelines by post from most print magazines. Send a large self-addressed envelope plus two IRCs.

Invest in an American–English dictionary. The quip that the US and the UK are 'divided by a common language' is not a myth – many spellings are different, as are some meanings, so don't risk getting caught out using a word or phrase that might not mean what you think it does. You can find some American magazines and newspapers on our newsstands. Read them – you need to familiarise yourself with current usage.

RED LIGHT

Since the attacks of 11th September 2001, American publishers are wary of any package from an unknown or unexpected source. You need to make an initial enquiry by e-mail, by letter or even by telephone. When you follow up your query, address your package clearly by name to the particular editor who agreed to look at it, and mark it 'requested submission'. *Do not send any kind of package without taking this precaution.*

Markets worldwide

With access to the Internet, you can find information about English-language markets all over the world. For example, key in 'English language magazines'. In seconds, you'll have leads to potential markets all over the world.

You can read the magazines online, see their guidelines, send article queries and book proposals by e-mail ... (Are you *still* wondering if it's worth getting a computer?)

The 'ex-pat' market

Don't overlook the magazines specifically produced for and by British people living abroad. Look at www.expatriates.com to see the range of markets open to English language contributions. Whatever your interests, you'll find at least one or two potential markets.

Recommended reading

Diana Cambridge, *How to Write for Magazines ... in One Weekend.*
Nicholas Corder, *Successful Non-Fiction Writing – A Guide to Getting Published.*
Adele Ramet, *Writing for Magazines.*
Michelle Ruberg (ed.), *Writer's Digest Handbook of Magazine Article Writing.*
Writer's Market (American edition).

Now you should know:

◆ What it takes to write successful articles.
◆ How to find markets.
◆ How to analyse your target publications.
◆ The various article types.
◆ How to write a saleable article.
◆ How to sell your work.
◆ Where to find information about overseas markets.

8

Writing and Selling Short Stories

In an earlier edition of this book, we asked readers to complete a questionnaire about their writing interests. We were not surprised to find that short-story writing was favourite. What *did* surprise us was the extent of the short story's lead. It stood 20 percentage points above its nearest rival, the novel. It isn't hard, then, to see why the competition to get short stories published is so fierce.

In this chapter:

- stories that sell
- choosing a market
- analysing your market
- stories for the Small Press
- how to be your own editor.

Other than those in a few popular magazines aimed at women readers, short stories don't sell well – even to writers who want to get their own stories published. Short story collections sell poorly, too, even those by famous writers. Yet the competition to get short stories published is as keen as ever. To succeed, then, you need more than talent and luck.

Don't be put off, though, by writers who complain that 'You can't sell short stories these days – editors don't want them ...' Comments like this are usually made by writers who don't – or won't – recognise the real situation. While it's true that there are fewer markets for short stories these days, the magazines that publish them can't get enough of the well written, entertaining, satisfying short stories their readers want.

STORIES THAT SELL

Every day, editorial desks groan under dull, clichéd, sermonising stories, lifeless, formless, pointless stories, sad, sordid, despairing stories... Editors don't want them. Their readers don't want them.

To be commercially successful, you need to combine creativity with pragmatism, taking a professional and analytical approach to writing and selling your stories.

A good short story needs:

- A single storyline, without subplots.
- Three or four characters at most.
- A single viewpoint, or two at most.
- A short time-scale.
- Consistent mood, tone and pace.
- Consistent writing style.
- Appropriate language.
- Brief descriptions.
- Minimum background.
- Concise dialogue.
- No lengthy preamble.
- No contrived ending.
- No preachy message.

> **— WISE WORDS —**
>
> You can learn how to do it. Read books on the craft. Read, study and analyse published short stories by today's successful writers.

Let's look at some aspects of short-story writing that seem to trouble many new writers:

Finding plots

Every plot begins with an idea. And ideas are everywhere. They're all around you – and inside you, too. Asked where she got her ideas, fantasy author Ursula

Le Guin wrote (in the American magazine *The Writer*), 'I don't get them, I am them; a writer's life is her ideas, her work, her words.'

Try this: every day for a week, read your daily and weekend newspapers from cover to cover, advertisements and all, and clip out *every* item that arouses even the mildest interest. Letters to the editor, reviews, the life-style sections, financial and sports pages as well as news stories – skip nothing. Collect anything that intrigues.

TIP FROM THE TOP

Stella Whitelaw, a highly successful writer of short stories, gave us this tip at one of her seminars: read the lists of runners on the racing pages; they are packed with intriguing names that could give you ideas and titles for stories.

Then browse through these cuttings, letting your imagination run free ... What made that young girl so desperate that she left an apparently happy and comfortable home to live rough on city streets? Why did that householder go to such lengths to prevent his neighbour uprooting a dying section of their commonly owned hedge? How did that woman fare when she returned to her job after winning her case for unfair dismissal? Would being 'Slimmer of the Year' change a man's life more than it would a woman's? What if ... and what if ...?

Keep a notebook with you at all times – the germ of an idea might bubble up in your brain at the most unexpected moment. Don't lose it.

Viewpoint

This is simply the point of view from which the story is told, that is, through the eyes of the hero or heroine or any other character, either in the first person or third person, or by an 'omniscient' storyteller who sees and hears everything.

It's best to tell your story through the eyes of one lead character. This helps to hold your story together by giving it a single emotional focus. There isn't room in a short story to introduce more than one viewpoint – this would diffuse the emotional effect and weaken the story.

You'll find it a useful exercise to take one of your stories and write it two or three times, from the viewpoints of different characters. Does the story work better from one viewpoint than from another? Is it more convincing? More intriguing? More exciting? Can you analyse *why*?

Then you need to decide whether first- or third-person narrative would serve your story best. This might be simply a matter or taste and suitability, or it could be dictated by the preferences of your target market. If you opt for first-person narrative, be careful not to fall into the trap of 'The Big "I" syndrome', where there is hardly a line without 'I', 'me', my', 'myself' or 'mine'. Many stories are ruined by this ineptitude, which can make even an exciting story boring and repetitive. Take a highlighter and mark every instance of 'I' etc. – you'll soon see if you've overburdened your story in this way.

CHOOSING A MARKET

We'll look at a few here, to give you a start. Then you must dig them out for yourself, from your newsagent's shelves, writers' magazines, the *Writers' & Artists' Yearbook* and *The Writer's Handbook*. Look out for new publications appearing on the newsstands. Read the *Press Gazette* to keep up with new launches.

Look beyond the obvious outlets. Search among specialist and hobby magazines – some will consider short fiction relevant to their subject. Some regional magazines and newspapers publish short stories, too.

TIP FROM THE TOP

Della Galton, a prolific writer of stories for women's magazines, offers these words of wisdom:

> The best advice I could give to anyone who wants to be published is to study your market. It sounds boring, but in my experience it's the key to success. Persistence helps, of course, but it's no good being persistent if you are writing stories that don't suit the

editor's requirements. I firmly believe that if you can write well and you target your market intelligently you will get your work into print sooner or later.

Women's magazines

This is the biggest paying market for short stories. You don't have to be a woman to write for them. You don't even have to write 'women's' stories. Some editors prefer male writers to adopt a feminine pen name, but masculine bylines appear more often these days.

Publishers D. C. Thomson are very helpful to promising new writers. They're always keen to find writers who can supply the right kind of fiction for their publications, which include *My Weekly, People's Friend* and *Weekly News*. They also need serial stories for the weekly magazines, and short romantic or romantic-suspense novels, 25–30,000 words long, for My Weekly Story Library and for the People's Friend Pocket Novel series.

The fiction editor of D. C. Thomson offers this advice:

> D. C. Thomson are always in the market to find good new writers for their wide range of publications, as shown by the many different leaflets we provide.
>
> New writers have to face the fact that competition for success is fierce. Because of the volume of contributions received, encouragement of new writers can only go to those who show most promise in producing our kind of material.
>
> Once you have studied the market, send your story to the editor of the magazine at which it is aimed or to the Central Fiction Department which acts as a clearing-house for unsolicited contributions.

Note the phrases: 'our kind of material' and 'once you have studied the market'. You have to show not only better than average writing ability, but also an awareness of the company's needs. They offer encouragement and advice, *not* tuition in writing. D. C. Thomson will supply their guideline leaflets on request – send a large SAE. The leaflets include writing for their women's magazines, for My Weekly Story Library and for children's and teenage picture- and photo-story scripts, and give details of how to submit your work.

— WISE WORDS —

It's a big mistake to tell an editor that the story you're offering is 'better' than those he is currently publishing. Editors of successful magazines know what their readers want.

ANALYSING YOUR MARKET

Get guidelines if you can, either by post or via the Internet. They'll give you a magazine's basic requirements. You'll increase your chances many times over, though, if you study your target market in close detail for yourself.

Collect *at least* six issues of your target magazine – a glance through one or two copies is not enough. Look only at recent issues, not old copies you might find in your dentist's waiting room or in a charity shop. Read again the advice in Chapter 7 on 'How to analyse a magazine'. You need a clear picture of the magazine's readership and the overall tone and style of its content.

Now concentrate on the short stories:

◆ How many words? The guidelines might specify '750 to 2,500 words', but you might find that most of the published stories are either 1,000 or 1,500 words, with only one or two as short as 750 words or as long as 2,500 words. You could have a better chance if you submit stories in the more favoured lengths.

◆ In which 'person' is the story told? First person? Third person? Is there a mix? If *all* the stories in your sample issues are written in first person, don't waste your time sending in a third-person viewpoint story. A mix of viewpoints might suggest that the editor has no strong preferences, but it could be worth assessing which viewpoint is used most. Note: very few mainstream short stories are told in second person.

◆ What type of stories appear most often? Romantic? Mysterious? Suspenseful? 'Twist-in-the-tail'? Spooky? Other?

◆ How many main characters per story?

◆ How many stories are written from a female's viewpoint? How many from a male's?

◆ In what age group are most of the main characters?

◆ Do the main characters have anything in common? Are they mostly single? Married? Widowed? Divorced? Living as partners?

◆ What kind of names do they have? 'Everyday'? Or 'posh'?

◆ What kind of occupations do they have? Housewives? Shopworkers? Secretaries? Teachers? Manual workers? Media workers? Models? Self-employed? High-flyers?

◆ What kind of relationships feature most often? Harmonious? Difficult? Stable? Shaky? New? Settled?

◆ What type of backgrounds appear to be favoured? Town? Country? Exotic? Prosaic?

◆ Do most stories feature love scenes? How explicit are these?

◆ How do most stories begin? With descriptive narrative? With dialogue? With action?

◆ How do most stories end? Happily? Loose ends tied up? Hopeful? Satisfactory? Teasing? Uplifting? Leaving readers to draw their own conclusions?

Every editor lives in hope of finding a wonderful story in the morning post. The more you know about your target publication, the better your chances of making an editor's day.

— WISE WORDS —

Keep your writing style simple and straightforward. Avoid any kind of contrived style or language that might intrude between your reader and what you want to tell him or her. Write to express, not to impress.

STORIES FOR THE SMALL PRESS

The Small Press plays a significant part in nurturing our country's writing talent. Other than competitions, who else will welcome our quirky, off-the-wall short stories, our experimental poetry? Who else will publish cutting-edge writers without fear of alienating shareholders, corporate boardrooms or big-money advertisers? Small Press editors publish what they like – and what they like is original, innovative prose and poetry, the kind that might not be welcomed in the high-powered commercialism of the world's IPCs and EMAPs.

There's a downside to independence, of course: the problem of funding. A few magazines receive Arts Council grants, some are stocked by larger bookshops, but most survive entirely on subscriptions. They're nearly always produced on a minimal budget by a single enthusiast or a small team working in their spare time and relying on reciprocal advertising for publicity. Many now only publish online, where they struggle for attention among hundreds of other small enterprises.

Every editor I know gives the same advice: 'Read the magazine you want to write for.' There is never a shortage of writers wanting to contribute material. Competition is tough, so you need to know what the editor likes.

Small Press magazines can do a lot for new writers who have yet to find their niche or make their mark in the literary world. Many have status beyond the Small Press world, and quite a few writers who got their start there continue to support them and to contribute work for little reward.

DID YOU KNOW?
William Boyd, Graham Swift and Ben Okri all had early works published in the Small Press.

Independent magazines receive far more submissions than they could possibly use, yet only the most successful can afford more than a token payment, and many can only offer complimentary copies. Writers themselves could do much to improve this situation. The arithmetic is simple: if every writer who wants to get published in the Small Press actually *bought* a magazine, there would be hundreds more markets able to pay what good writing deserves. Wouldn't we all benefit from that?

Study these markets, too
Always study *at least* one issue of a magazine before you submit any work. You need to digest its style and flavour. Not every magazine will suit you, of course, so search out those that do.

You don't have to commit yourself to a subscription – most magazines will sell you a single copy on request. But *please don't* ask or expect them to hand out free samples. These small businesses struggle to survive – they can't afford to subsidise your market. Remember, too, *always* to enclose an SAE with every submission or query.

Light's List offers a huge choice of Small Press magazines worldwide. See page 173.

HOW TO BE YOUR OWN EDITOR
Do revise and rewrite. Objective self-criticism is a skill worth cultivating. These are the main faults and weaknesses to look for – they might cause your story to be rejected:

1. Is the opening too long? Too slow? Too general? It's vital to grab the reader from the opening paragraph.

2. Have you begun in the right place, at an intriguing point in the action?

Avoid the leisurely preamble – you don't have wordage to waste. Get straight into the story.

3. Have you used flashback? Too much 'history' can kill your story's pace.

4. Have you developed your characters and portrayed them through their actions, reactions and interactions rather than by bald exposition?

5. Have you sustained momentum throughout, moving the story on through cause and effect? Or have you cluttered the narrative with unnecessary detail and superfluous characters? Your hero might be reminded of his good fortune when he sees a beggar, but we don't need to know how Betty the Baglady fell on hard times. Keep the focus where it belongs.

6. Is the ending satisfying, believable, and logical in the story's own terms? Or did you run out of steam, leave loose ends, or introduce a contrived 'twist' or a new character who provides all the answers?

7. Is the viewpoint consistent? The tiniest shift can destroy the reader's empathy. She won't realise consciously what has happened, but her involvement with the story will have been weakened. For example, your hero sees his lost love: 'David's heart began to thump, and tears welled up in his blue eyes...' The single word 'blue' is an observation *from the outside*, requiring us to *look at* David rather than *feel with* him.

8. Have you given your characters suitable names? Take care not to 'place' your characters in inappropriate age bands or social categories: 'Ada and Herbert', 'Tracey and Kev', 'Camilla and Peregrine' – names like these evoke different perceptions and expectations.

9. Is the dialogue natural? Or does it seem stilted and unconvincing? Read it aloud, into a tape if possible, and listen for awkward phrases and out-of-character speech patterns and vocabulary. Use abbreviations – 'couldn't', he'd', 'they'll', and so on – where they feel right.

10. Have you left your reader space to use his imagination – or have you described every move, thought and feeling? We don't need to know every detail of every scene. Don't be afraid of 'jumps' in time and place – they can

lend pace to your story by cutting out any passages the reader might be tempted to skip.

11. Is your spelling sound? Careless spelling can alter or fog your meaning, and gives the editor negative messages about you. Don't rely on your computer program's spell-check facility – it can't distinguish errors like 'there' instead of 'their', 'holed' instead of 'hold' and the like.

12. And your punctuation? Careless punctuation can produce nonsense: 'The rain was pouring down Carol' does not mean the same as 'The rain was pouring down, Carol'.

13. And your syntax? Syntax is the ordering of words to convey a clear and unambiguous meaning. Read this: 'The mayor arrived to light the bonfire with his wife.' The right words are there, but their order makes the statement absurd. Make sure you've said what you meant to say.

14. Are your tenses consistent? It's all too easy to shift from present to past and vice versa without noticing.

15. Is your writing concise and sharp? Or wordy and slack? Tight writing has more impact. Especially, avoid weak verbs that need supporting adverbs, as in: a branch *fell heavily* to the ground – try *thudded.*

16. Have you used *active* rather than *passive* verbs? 'Fido chased Felix' (active) is stronger than 'Felix was chased by Fido' (passive).

17. Have you avoided vagueness? 'A crowd was waiting to see the parade' is woolly. 'Crowds waited ten-deep along the parade route' is more vivid.

18. Is your text repetitive? Don't bore your reader with 'Mary's mother said this' and 'Mary's mother said that', 'Suddenly this' and 'Suddenly that'. Vary your vocabulary.

Recommended reading

Damon Knight, *Creating Short Fiction.*
John Light (ed.), *Light's List.*
Margaret Lucke, *Schaum's Quick Guide to Writing Short Stories.*
Iain Pattison, *Cracking the Short Story Market.*

Stella Whitelaw, *How to Write Short Short Stories*.

Now you should know:

- ◆ What makes a saleable short story.
- ◆ How to choose and analyse a market.
- ◆ What opportunities the Small Press offers.
- ◆ How to criticise and edit your own work.

9

Writing and Selling Your First Novel

To bring a novel from inception to publication can take two or three years. Publishers have to think ahead. So does the smart writer. Don't waste your time trying to cash in on today's bestsellers. Publishers don't want clones of the novels they've just published, however successful. As a newcomer, your best chance lies in writing the novel you're burning to write, the story that will stand out in its passion and sincerity. There is only one rule: don't bore your reader.

In this chapter:

♦ getting to know the book business
♦ the different types of novel
♦ checking your manuscript for fatal flaws
♦ preparing your submission package
♦ marketing your novel.

GETTING TO KNOW THE BOOK BUSINESS

Read the weekly trade 'bible', *The Bookseller*. It's the nearest you'll get to a crystal ball, with its listings of books that will be published over the following three to six months. Subscriptions are not cheap, although they give you access to daily news updates and a 'Publications of the Week' listing on the *Bookseller* website. If you make friends with your local bookshop (and you should) they might let you browse through their copies.

The weekly *Publishing News* is cheaper, though not so comprehensive.

Read the 'Books' pages in the weekend papers, too. They often include book trade information and news (and the odd bit of gossip).

— **WISE WORDS** —

The more you read about the book business, the more information you'll absorb and remember. In this business, knowledge is power.

THE DIFFERENT TYPES OF NOVEL

In most writing manuals, you'll see references to 'general' or 'mainstream' and 'genre' or 'category' fiction. Publishers 'label' novels for ease of reference in catalogues, bookstores and libraries.

These are the main fiction categories:

◆ General – a huge variety that includes 'literary' fiction and any other kind of novel that doesn't fit easily into a category.
◆ Action-adventure.
◆ Historical.
◆ Mystery, which includes 'crime'.
◆ Romance.
◆ Science fiction, which includes 'fantasy' and 'horror'.
◆ Short stories – collections from individual authors and anthologies, in book form.
◆ Thrillers.
◆ War.
◆ Westerns.
◆ Graphic novels and manga.

These listings include any and every combination of the above types – you could write sci-fi Westerns, romantic thrillers, historical action-adventure ... Don't let any thoughts of 'fitting into a category' stifle your imagination. Go with whatever inspires you.

There are also 'graphic' versions of many of the above categories, from 'The Simpsons' to Shakespeare. These are stories told as pictures-plus-captions, like the children's picture-stories described in Chapter 11 but aimed at an older market.

Graphic novels and the Japanese-inspired 'manga' picture-stories are becoming increasingly popular. Look at these in the bookshops and on the Internet – you might enjoy telling stories in graphic form.

Genre fiction

This is a blanket term applied to fiction that falls into the most easily recognised categories. The most popular genre types are:

♦ **Romance**: most major publishers include romantic fiction in their lists. The term 'romance' covers a wide range of novels, including love stories, historical romance, romantic-suspense, romantic-fantasy ....

TIP FROM THE TOP

Jean Saunders, best-selling author of romantic fiction who also writes under the names 'Rowena Summers' and 'Rachel Moore', advises:

> Don't think of romantic fiction as being the soft option. It has come of age in recent years, competition is fierce and it pays to read as many current novels in the genre as you can. Have a story to tell, with an interesting background. Most of all, create intelligent and appealing characters who have the motivation and gumption to achieve their goals. Plan your story so that there are plenty of twists to keep the reader reading. Your aim is to be a page-turner, so remember two vital words to keep the story moving – conflict and pace.

♦ **Crime, mystery and thrillers**: most major publishers have crime, mystery and thriller lists, and they'll snap up a good original story, especially if you can create a character or characters who could inspire a series. Michael Connelly's 'Harry Bosch', Reginald Hill's 'Dalziel and Pascoe', Ian Rankin's 'Rebus', for example, are the kind of steady sellers that publishers love.

To write successful modern crime stories, you need to keep up to date with developments in detection methods – DNA, computerised databanks and so on – to make obvious mistakes would damage your credibility. On the other hand, don't be so earnest that you forget that you're writing a story for people to read for relaxation and entertainment. You're not writing a forensic textbook. You could, of course, set your novel in earlier times, before detection became such a sophisticated science. Andrew Taylor, for one, enjoys great success with his 'Lydmouth' novels, set in the 1950s.

TIP FROM THE TOP

Stella Whitelaw, author of the successful 'Jordan Lacey' novels, offers this advice:

The vital element of crime writing is that it is fiction based on fact. Write the genre that you like to read, whether a spy thriller, private eye, forensic, police procedural, war crime, cosy crime, adventure. The different styles are endless.

Find a strong theme with believable characters. Cull the newspapers for crime stories. Become friends with a policeman/detective to check procedures and watch *The Bill* for cop dialogue. Make procedure believable even if it is not strictly accurate.

Complete your novel before you try to sell it

If you've never written a novel before, you would be wise to complete your manuscript *before* you approach the market. In today's fast-moving publishing world, few editors and agents are willing to work with a new author on the basis of an outline and sample. You must be able to show you can deliver what you promise.

Writing a whole novel takes a lot of stamina and probably a lot more time than you think. You want to be in a position to respond quickly if an agent or editor likes your submission package and asks you to send the whole novel. If you still have months of work to do on it, you might lose your chance.

CHECKING YOUR MANUSCRIPT FOR FATAL FLAWS

Put your manuscript away for at least a couple of weeks, then read it again right through, asking:

1. Have you kept the spotlight on your basic theme and main characters? Sub-plots and minor characters should not overshadow these.

2. Have you developed your characters fully, portraying them through their actions, reactions and interactions, and keeping them 'in character' throughout? Don't let them act out of character without a good reason.

3. Has your protagonist changed (or been changed) by the end? A main character who neither changes nor grows in some meaningful way between the first and last pages will be static and unconvincing.

4. Is your story logical? Even a fantasy needs to make sense within its own terms.

5. Does the story maintain a satisfactory 'cause and effect' sequence, with each event following on logically from what has gone before? A plot that relies on coincidence, for example, or the convenient arrival of a new character will strain your reader's belief in your story. Coincidences do happen in real life, but they are seldom convincing in fiction.

> ### — WISE WORDS —
>
> Avoid coincidences in your plot – they'll strain your reader's credulity and make him feel cheated.

6. Have you kept control of your chosen narrative voice (or voices) throughout? Check for unintentional switches or slips of viewpoint.

7. Does every scene take the action forward, enrich characterisation, increase tension, or provide a calming or reflective interlude? If it does none of these, ask yourself why it's there. Could it be cut without harming the story?

> ### — WISE WORDS —
>
> Discard any passages you suspect your reader might be tempted to skip.

8. Check every piece of dialogue – is it 'in character'? Does it contribute to characterisation and/or move the story forward?

9. Have you been sparing with description and explanation, leaving room for your reader's imagination to come into play?

10. Is the writing strong, evoking all the senses? Have you used the passive voice where the active voice would work better? Have you used 'to be' verbs supported by adverbs where strong verbs alone would be more effective? Flabby writing can ruin the impact of the most brilliant story.

11. Look again at the story as a whole. Is the structure balanced? Have you begun in the right place? Don't jeopardise your chances by starting the story too early, providing too much background and taking too long to get things moving. Many a story has been saved by cutting out the first chapter and plunging straight into the action.

12. Have you sustained momentum through the middle section, moving the story on through cause and effect, action and reaction, tightening tension as you build to the climax?

13. Have you left your reader feeling satisfied that the whole story has been told? Make sure you haven't left any unintentional loose ends.

14. Are you absolutely sure your novel is as good as you can make it?

PREPARING YOUR SUBMISSION PACKAGE

Whether you plan to send your work to an agent or straight to a publisher, you need to prepare a submission package. An agent or editor must be able to assess your novel quickly and easily. *Never* send your complete ms till you're asked to do so.

Look at the agent or publisher's entry in the yearbook and look, too, at their website for information on how they like to be approached. Do your homework on other authors in whom they have an interest and mention any you admire.

Have your submission package ready before you make your first contact. Your package should consist of:

♦ A covering letter addressed to the agent or editor *by name*. Show them you selected them with care and not by sticking a pin in the *Writers' & Artists' Yearbook*. If you're aiming for a series, indicate that you have other ideas in preparation. If your novel is a 'stand-alone', leave that part out. Don't offer either your own or anyone else's opinion of the story. Only the agent or editor's opinion matters. (See Figures 9 and 10.)

Dear Hope Hitfinder

I write to ask if you would be interested in representing my mystery novel 'Did He Fall?', complete at 90,000 words. A second novel featuring the same main characters is already in outline and I have ideas for future titles.

I am approaching you because you represent several authors, including 'X, Y and Z', whose work I admire.

Mystery and crime novels have always been my favourite reading, and I believe 'Did He Fall?' would fit well into the mystery genre.

I enclose a brief blurb, biographies of the four main characters, a synopsis, the first two chapters and my author biography.

Sincerely

Millie Author

Figure 9. Example of a covering letter for a novel submission to an agent.

Dear Barry Editor

I write to ask if you will consider my mystery novel 'Did He Fall?' for publication. The novel is complete at 90,000 words. A second novel featuring the same main characters is already in outline and I have ideas for further titles.

I am approaching you because you have published several books I've enjoyed, particularly 'A' by 'B' and 'X' by 'Z'. I believe 'Did He Fall?' could suit your list.

I enclose a brief blurb, biographies of the four main characters, a synopsis, the first two chapters and my author biography.

Sincerely

Millie Author

Figure 10. Example of a covering letter for a novel submission to a publisher.

◆ A *brief* blurb, no more than two or three paragraphs. The blurb is intended to *sell* the story, in the same way as the blurb on the cover of a published novel sells it to the prospective reader. (See Figure 11.)

'Did He Fall?' blurb:

Former police detective-inspector Jake McKinlay believes he has left his bad times behind. He has moved to the city where his ex-wife and young daughter now live, and has made peace with them. Unwittingly, he puts his hopes of a possible reconciliation at risk when he agrees to help his ex-wife's friend Laura Canning investigate the death of her uncle, impresario Max Laurence. Laura believes Max did not drown by accident and that there has been a cover-up.

Jake finds himself attracted to Laura and, through her, he is drawn into the strange world of Max's family, where undercurrents of tension grow as he uncovers long-hidden secrets someone in the family is desperate to keep concealed. The deeper he probes the more dangerous the secrets he uncovers, until he finds himself, Laura, and his own child in mortal peril.

Figure 11. Example of a 'selling' blurb.

◆ Brief biographies of your most important characters, no more than one or two paragraphs for each character. Think these out carefully – it's essential to show that your characters have the potential to make readers care about them. (See Figure 12.)

'Did He Fall?' main character biographies:

Jake McKinlay, 42, just under six feet tall, physically slim and strong, but walks with a slight limp, legacy of the incident that got him prematurely 'retired' from the police force. Always a maverick, he drank too much and sometimes strayed across the line of legality in his investigations. Doesn't work now, but stays sober the hard way, without any support network.

Loves blues music and Western films. Divorced but renting a flat from his ex-wife above the pet store she owns. Still cares for her and adores his eight-year-old daughter Amy. Now making the first moves towards setting up as a private investigator.

Laura Canning, 35, mother of a ten-year-old daughter. Medium height, slim, dark-haired. Professional photo-journalist specialising in theatre. Living apart from her husband, having moved back to her family home to consider her future. The failure of her marriage has severely dented her self-confidence and she is afraid to trust her own judgement about Max's death.

Figure 12. Examples of character biographies.

◆ A concise synopsis of the whole novel, written in the present tense. Touch on key scenes, making clear which is your main character, what their ultimate goal is, who and what stands between them and that goal. Show how the story ends. New writers often try to conceal the ending in an attempt to intrigue. This is a big mistake. The agent or editor needs to be able to assess the story as a whole. (See Figure 13.)

'Did He Fall?' synopsis:

As he begins to settle into his new home in the historic city of York, life is looking up for Jake McKinlay. At last he feels he is getting his life into some kind of order following years of fighting his drinking habit while scraping a living any way he could after getting compulsorily if discreetly 'retired' from his job as a detective inspector in Glasgow CID.

Today, he has thrown the windows open to the spring sunshine and is starting to hang his treasured collection of Western film posters, feeling at last that it's worth making the small flat look as if he might be staying for a while.

He is pleased when his ex-wife, Sally, rings him from the pet shop she runs on the ground floor of the building. He is trying very hard to repair some of the damage he has caused in their lives. Sally brings her friend Laura Canning up to his flat, where he is brewing a pot of coffee to welcome them. Sally asks Jake a favour on Laura's behalf. Will Jake use his experience as a detective to look into what Laura maintains is the suspicious death of her uncle, Max Laurence?

Jake agrees, mainly to please Sally but also because he finds Laura's arguments logical and convincing. His curiosity is aroused, and he finds he is almost eager to put his detection skills, too long unused, into practice again.

Jake accompanies Laura and Sally to Max Laurence's funeral and afterwards to the family home of Laura's parents where he meets several other relatives and becomes aware of tension simmering in the air. The house is mansion-sized and the family well dressed, but Jake notices the threadbare curtains, worn carpets and the washed-to-death table linen.

Figure 13. Part of a synopsis for a novel, 'Did He Fall?'
© Chriss McCallum.

> **RED LIGHT**
> It's the mark of an amateur to conceal the ending. This won't intrigue
> either agent or editor – it will simply annoy them.

♦ The *first* two or three chapters (about 50 manuscript pages). Take time to make these as good as you possibly can – they must capture their reader's interest *from the first page*, as well as showing your writing and storytelling ability.

♦ Your author biography, a page at most. Include anything about yourself and your life that makes you interesting and potentially saleable as an author.

♦ Sufficient return postage.

It's acceptable these days to offer your novel to more than one publisher or agent at the same time *unless* they specifically state that they won't look at multiple submissions.

And when you're eventually offered a contract, apply to join the Society of Authors. The *offer* makes you eligible for membership, and the society will check the contract for you *before you sign it*.

Here are a few tips about contacting agents and editors:

♦ *Do* address your letter and your package to an agent or editor *by name*.

♦ *Do* keep your letter succinct, to the point, and preferably not longer than one page.

♦ *Do* be professional. Your letter should be written in a tone that is confident but neither arrogant nor fawning.

♦ *Do* check your grammar, spelling, punctuation and syntax. If you send out the message that you can't be bothered to write an immaculate letter, neither agent nor editor is going to trust you to deliver a competent manuscript.

◆ *Don't* try to be funny – unless you're offering a humorous novel, in which case be very sure any humour you demonstrate in your letter really *is* funny, otherwise you could kill your chances there and then.

◆ *Don't* tell the recipient how much he's going to enjoy your novel because your auntie loves it and your best friend says it's the best thing he's ever read. Let the agent or editor make up his own mind.

◆ *Don't* attempt to tease by concealing your novel's ending. Agents and editors need to know you're going to deliver an ending that will satisfy the reader.

TIP FROM THE TOP

Speaking at a conference, novelist Celia Brayfield told us that while she was writing her novel *Pearls*, she cut out the *Sunday Times* bestseller list every week and pasted her name and the title of her novel at the number one position. She then pinned up the list above her writing desk, where it inspired her every day.

Recommended reading
Carole Blake, *From Pitch to Publication.*
Celia Brayfield, *Bestseller.*
Sarah Harrison, *How to Write a Blockbuster 'and Make Millions'.*
Janet Laurence, *Writing Crime Fiction.*
Betsy Lerner, *An Editor's Advice to Writers – The Forest for the Trees.*
Evan Marshall, *Novel Writing – 16 Steps to Success.*
David Morrell, *Lessons From a Lifetime of Writing – A Novelist Looks at his Craft.*
Marina Oliver, *Writing Historical Fiction.*
Jean Saunders, *The Craft of Writing Romance.*
Jean Saunders, *How to Create Fictional Characters.*
Jean Saunders, *How to Plot Your Novel.*
Jean Saunders, *How to Research Your Novel.*
Jean Saunders, *How to Write Realistic Dialogue.*
Stella Whitelaw, *How to Write & Sell a Book Proposal.*
Stella Whitelaw, *How to Write & Sell a Synopsis.*

Now you should know:

- Your choice of novel types.
- How to check your manuscript's readiness for submission.
- How to prepare your submission package.
- How to market your novel.

$$\binom{10}{}$$

Writing and Selling Non-Fiction Books

Are you an expert on a subject that would interest a large number of people? Do you have first-hand experience or knowledge that might benefit, profit, amuse, intrigue or inspire others? Have you set up and run a successful business? Built your own house? Walked round the coast of Britain? Prospected for gold in the Andes? Perhaps you're already thinking about writing a book but don't know where to begin.

In this chapter:

- assessing your idea
- first find your publisher
- preparing a proposal
- approaching a publisher
- writing specialist non-fiction.

ASSESSING YOUR IDEA

Before you commit yourself to the project and all the hard work it will involve, ask yourself:

1. Is the subject big enough for a book? *An Encyclopaedia of Houseplant Care* would be. *How to Water Your Aspidistra* would not.

2. Would the subject interest a wide enough readership to make it a commercial proposition? Books do get written and published on some pretty obscure topics, but these are usually intended for a specialist market. It depends on how wide a readership you want to reach, and on whether it's mainly profit or prestige you want. Many publishers might want *An A–Z of Microwave Cookery*, but few would take on, for instance, *Advanced Theory of Semiconductors*.

3. Will the subject attract the book-buying public as well as library stockists? The biggest potential sales are in books on self-improvement (both physical and psychological), health, food and diet, leisure activities and hobbies. Do-it-yourself titles sell well, and books on cookery and gardening waltz off the shelves. 'How-to' books are in constant demand, especially those that show how to make or save money or how to lose weight.

— WISE WORDS —

An American publisher, asked by a novice writer if he thought anyone would ever write the 'Great American Novel', advised: 'Forget the Great American Novel. What this country needs is a good book on how to repair your own car.'

You've got a suitable subject – so how do you tackle it?

First, break it down into manageable sections. The prospect of getting 30,000 words or more down on paper can be pretty daunting. Split into ten or twelve chapters of 3,000 words, it loses much of its terror – you can think of it as a series of articles.

Divide your subject on paper, then, into ten or twelve sub-themes. These will form your chapters. Under each sub-theme heading note all the information you already have relevant to that section. Note any obvious gaps in the information. You'll have to do some research to fill those gaps.

Now comes the crunch

Do you have, or do you know how and where to find, enough material to write each of your chapters *without waffle or padding*? Can you realistically expect to pack every chapter with interesting and relevant information?

If not, abandon it, and look for a more substantial subject. Don't throw away your notes, though. You've probably got enough material there for several articles at least.

If you're sure you have enough material for a book, go ahead and prepare your proposal.

FIRST FIND YOUR PUBLISHER

Don't write the book yet. If you don't find a taker, you don't want to have wasted your time writing an unsaleable book. And if a publisher does express an interest, he might want to make suggestions about the way you write the book – perhaps a different kind of treatment from the one you originally envisaged, or a format to fit an existing list. If you had already written the book you would have to do an extensive rewrite.

PREPARING A PROPOSAL

Make an outline of the whole book.

1. Set down your title. The publisher might want to change it, but for the purposes of the proposal you need a working title. Make it as snappy as you can. *Raising Funds for Charity* is more effective than *Organising Events to Raise Money for Charitable Projects*. It would fit the spine of the book better, too.

2. Write down your chapter headings and set out underneath them, briefly, all the points you'll deal with in each chapter.

3. This will give you the skeleton of your book, the bones on which you'll build the meat.

4. Type the outline neatly in single spacing, like a letter – this is a document, not a working typescript. An extract from such a document is shown in Figure 14. Indicate the proposed overall length of the book (its 'extent'). If illustrations are appropriate, say whether or not you can supply them. The publisher will advise you if he prefers to make arrangements for illustrations himself.

Overview: *Raising Funds for Charity*

The book will cover all aspects of fund-raising, from individual efforts (making and selling crafts, holding a coffee morning, hosting a sales party and so on) to larger committee-run business-sponsored events like dinner-dances and concerts.

It will be spiced with accounts of real-life achievements – I know of a man who raised many thousands of pounds by hiring Concorde and flying a party to New York – which will intrigue, encourage and inspire the reader.

Legal, health and safety aspects will all be covered. There will be suggestions for a comprehensive range of money-making possibilities and a directory of contact addresses: services, suppliers, information sources and so on.

I believe that there are many people who would be attracted by having so much information offered in one handy volume. It will appeal to individuals and to organisations: clubs and societies, schools and colleges, hospital support groups, church groups and many more.

As far as I have been able to ascertain, there are very few publications on the open market that gather together so many facts and suggestions and combine them with an interesting and entertaining narrative.

And one of the essential ingredients for success in any enterprise is surely that the participants should enjoy the venture from the outset. The necessary literature should be part of the enjoyment.

Format:

I plan to structure the book in three sections. Briefly,

1. Setting up, forming a committee, and investigating legal matters.
2. Planning strategies and events.
3. A digest of fund-raising ideas.

Plus: Contact addresses, sources of information, useful publications and an index.

Part of an outline for a proposed book *Raising Funds for Charity*.

Introduction
A short general overview of the choices for raising funds as an individual, a small group or a larger committee-run group. It will also draw attention to the need to know how the law affects various activities – to be covered in one of the chapters.

Chapter 1: How to set up a committee
Showing the various offices – chairperson, secretary, treasurer and so on – and defining each office and the responsibilities it carries, stressing the importance of allocating the right job to the right person. For instance, it's hopeless to appoint as treasurer someone who can't tell an invoice from a receipt.

Chapter 2: Fund raising and the law
What you need to know about what you can do without permission, what you need permission for – for instance, you can't sell raffle tickets door-to-door without a special permit – and what you can't do at all.

Chapter 3: Drawing up a provisional programme of events
Your committee needs to decide what is within its members' capabilities and what isn't. For instance, there's no point in trying to organise a jumble sale if your members are not prepared to sort out the jumble. It's no good, either, deciding to have a brass band concert if the nearest brass band is based a hundred miles away and you would have to meet its travelling expenses.

This chapter will include a list of suggestions for events: a summer fair, a Christmas craft fair, an antiques and collectables fair, a car boot sale, a raffle, an auction, a quiz night, a gala dinner and dozens more. It will also point out the areas where you need special insurance and safety precautions.

Figure 14. Overview and part of a chapter outline for a non-fiction book.

The sales pitch

On a separate sheet of paper, type out:

- A short, concise explanation of the book's purpose and area of interest.
- Why you believe there's a need for it.
- What market you see for it.
- What competition there is.
- Why you believe *your* book will be better.
- Why *you* are the right person to write this book.

APPROACHING A PUBLISHER

Look through the publishers listed in the *Writers' & Artists' Yearbook* and *The Writer's Handbook* and list those who specify an interest in the kind of book you're planning.

Next, check with Booktrust to see what other books on your topic are currently on the market and if any are due to be published in the near future.

Decide which publisher looks like the best prospect. Find out the name of the editor responsible for the type of book you want to offer, either by looking on their website or by ringing the switchboard. If the operator doesn't know, ask to be put through to the editorial department for non-fiction books. Ask there for the appropriate name and check the spelling. Don't try to discuss the book on the phone unless you are specifically asked to do so – all you want is the right name so your proposal will reach the right person. (*The Writer's Handbook* gives many editors' names in its listings, but check anyway – publishing personnel move about a lot.)

TIP FROM THE TOP

Here are ten essential points of advice from Graham Lawler, Managing Director of Studymates Limited, publishers of academic books and writer's guides:

1. *Do* check the publisher actually publishes your type of book.
2. *Do* find out the name of the contact.
3. *Do* send an SAE.

4. *Do* explain how your book will fit into their list (read some of their books).
5. *Do* explain how you are media friendly and keen to sell your book.
6. *Do* remember they are busy.
7. *Don't* pester with follow up calls.
8. *Don't* run down any other author in their list; they did choose to publish that author.
9. *Don't* use jargon.
10. *Don't* send unsolicited work if the company has said not to do so.

Your covering letter

This should be brief and to the point. All the information about your book is in the proposal, so there's no need to repeat it here.

If you have any special qualifications for writing the book, mention these – but only mention *relevant* matters. Your degree in metaphysics won't persuade an editor to accept your book on fund-raising – it has no relevance. Your experience in the field does, though. All you need is something similar to Figure 15.

Dear Mr Corn-Harvester

I enclose a proposal for a book about fund-raising for charity. I have 15 years of experience in this field, both in active organisation and in administration, and have published articles on the subject in *Fund-raising Fun* and *Charitable Times* (clips enclosed).

Will you please consider my proposed book for your list?

Yours sincerely

Figure 15. Example of a covering letter for a non-fiction book proposal.

Prepare a sample chapter or two

You might have to wait a while for a reply, or you might have to try several publishers before you get a nibble of interest. Spend this time working on a couple of sample chapters and on gathering information you're going to need to fill the gaps you identified when you made your original notes.

When a publisher does express interest, he'll probably ask you to send him at least one complete chapter to see whether or not the content will live up to the promise of the proposal. He'll also want to assess your capabilities as a writer before he commits himself, so you must make your sample as good as you possibly can.

When you're offered an agreement

If he likes your sample, the publisher will either ask to see the completed ms 'on spec' (in which case you should think very carefully before committing yourself to finishing the book with no definite prospect of acceptance) or he will offer you an agreement on the strength of what he has already seen. With the agreement, he might also offer you an advance against royalties.

The *offer* of a book contract entitles you to apply for membership of the Society of Authors, who will advise you about the agreement you've been offered, so as soon as you receive the document, contact them and they'll scrutinise it on your behalf *before you sign it.*

Recommended reading

Nicholas Corder, *Successful Non-Fiction Writing – A guide to Getting Published.*
Carole Blake, *From Pitch to Publication.*
Michael Legat, *Understanding Publishers' Contracts.*
Society of Authors, *Quick Guide to Publishing Contracts.*

WRITING SPECIALIST NON-FICTION

The range of non-fiction books is almost limitless. If you have any kind of specialist knowledge, think about putting it to use in print. The following are just a few of the areas you might look at.

Educational writing

You don't have to be a teacher to write educational material. Teaching experience helps, certainly, in preparing course material or textbooks, but the most important requirement is skill in communication.

The educational writer has to work within strict guidelines. Content, language and structure must be geared to specific ages and abilities. You can get information about courses and relevant syllabus material from local education authorities, career centres and libraries. If you are a teacher, you have an advantage over the 'outsider', because you're in touch with current needs.

There are openings, however, for those with no teaching experience at all. What you need is the ability to write well to specific guidelines.

English language teaching

The English language is taught all over the world, not only to children but to people of all ages. Most of this teaching is done with storybooks, not textbooks. Some of these are original stories, but many are adapted from modern novels and from the life stories of famous people – Marilyn Monroe, Charlie Chaplin, Sir Winston Churchill, Nelson Mandela ... Non-fiction subjects like airports, animals, earthquakes, volcanoes, the sinking of the *Titanic*, the Olympic Games and World Cup sport are popular, too.

What is required is a 'good read' to keep the learner turning the pages so he absorbs the language almost without thinking about it. These abridgements and adaptations have to be prepared within tight disciplines according to varying levels of ability. At the lower end, for example, you might work with:

◆ A given word list of, say, 300 words.
◆ A given list of simple sentence structures.
◆ Very simple tenses.

With these basic 'bricks', you build a story or, for an adaptation, you use the existing storyline.

If you think you could make a go of this kind of tightly disciplined writing, contact publishers who have an English Language Teaching (ELT) department, citing any relevant qualifications and writing experience, and pitch a few ideas for stories and/or adaptations.

Reference books

These can be a good publishing proposition because they are steady sellers. There are reference books on every imaginable subject, from wildflowers to monastery sewerage systems. If you have an idea for a reference book – perhaps you've spotted a gap in the market – and have enough knowledge of the subject to write it, approach a publisher with a proposal as outlined on pages 107–9.

The religious press

Book publishers and magazines catering for all religious denominations need inspirational and educational material. Most of the religious publications in the UK are related to the Christian faith in its various denominations. You'll find publishers of religious material listed in the *Writers' & Artists' Yearbook* and *The Writer's Handbook*. Many smaller religious groups publish their own books, papers and magazines. You're probably familiar with the publications and publishers relating to your own faith, but you might not have thought of them as markets for your writing.

Whatever your religious persuasion, however, you should apply the same basic principle for successful writing: study each publication as an individual market, because they are all different and will look for material that satisfies their particular outlook and interests.

Most cities and large towns have at least one religious bookshop, as do cathedrals and many of the larger churches countrywide. You can browse there and look for the publishers whose books reflect your own interests. If you buy one or two publications, so much the better – you could then enlist the shop staff's help for advice about appropriate publishers. Your library, too, should have information on religious publications, and most large bookstores have departments devoted to books on religions worldwide.

There is a society for writers of specifically Christian material, The Association of Christian Writers (see page 176).

Travel writing

Successful travel writing involves much more than descriptions of journeys and exotic locations or quoting from brochures and guide books. A travel article or book should:

♦ Provide insight into people's lives and culture.
♦ Create a sense of atmosphere.
♦ Bring a place to vivid life through details rather than generalities.
♦ Get the facts right, but treat them imaginatively.
♦ Be descriptive without being overloaded with superlatives, clichés and flowery adjectives.

Too many aspiring travel writers concentrate on descriptions of beautiful sights seen through the windows of their car or tourist coach. You need to spend time absorbing the local atmosphere, talking to the people, taking photographs and making on-the-spot notes of your impressions – not just what you see, but what you feel, hear and smell, what attracts, what repels, what arouses your curiosity. Dig beneath the surface, and be sensitive to the feelings of the local people.

If you need inspiration, don't turn to guide books or brochures – read Jonathan Raban, Eric Newby, Paul Theroux and the hugely successful Bill Bryson ... the best travel writers can transport the armchair traveller into the heart of another place, another culture. They make you feel the thin air of the Andes, see the grandeur of the Victoria Falls, smell the sweat that built the pyramids, hear the echo of the jackboot in the streets of Warsaw.

And don't forget the photographs. They could be vital in clinching a sale.

— **WISE WORDS** —

Travel writing has more in common with fiction than with journalism. It needs more than facts, figures and descriptions – it needs the pulse of life. If you can achieve this, you'll delight the editors who receive your mss.

Copywriting

Copywriting for business can be very lucrative. The main areas are advertising and direct mail. To get a feel for what's needed, stop skipping the adverts and binning your 'junk' mail. Somebody has been paid to write all that material, and paid very well. Maybe you could do it, too, and develop a useful sideline or even a new career writing copy designed to sell products and services.

You could start by offering your services to local companies. Study their promotional material. Could you write it better? Can you think of a more effective approach? If so, let them see your ideas. Present them in sharp persuasive language.

Whether you're writing press releases, adverts, sales literature, newsletters, posters or TV and radio commercials, you need to know how to construct good copy and avoid the pitfalls.

Your writing skills could help small businesses in particular to promote themselves more effectively and at less expense than could a large advertising company.

Recommended reading

Robert W. Bly, *The Copywriter's Handbook*.
J. Jonathan Gabay, *Teach Yourself Copywriting*.
Diana Wimbs, *Freelance Copywriting*.

Technical writing

To be a successful technical writer, you need many of the qualities and skills of an investigative journalist. You need to know how to sift essential information from masses of data, then present that information in terms that are easily understood by the people who need it.

To be a technical writer, you would need:

◆ To enjoy researching, possibly into subject matter you know little or nothing about, in enough depth to clarify the subject to people who need to understand it.

◆ To be skilled enough in human relationships to win cooperation from people who hold the information you need – you might have to apply a little psychology when you deal with a temperamental genius (or even worse, with someone who thinks he's a genius).

◆ To possess a logical mind and a good memory.

◆ To be able to present your findings in clear, concise, unambiguous English, without resort to specialist jargon.

It's that last point that prompts many businesses to employ writers from outside the company to prepare sales brochures, users' manuals and suchlike. Company employees can be too close to the subject to see that what is commonplace knowledge to them might be a complete mystery to the layman or non-technician. If you've ever torn your hair out over a computer handbook you'll recognise the problem. An 'outsider' sees the gaps and the areas of possible confusion because he needs to get them clear in his own mind before he can pass them on to his readers.

And a brief look at some others

◆ **Guide books**. If you know an area well, either at home or abroad, you might be able to create a guide to help other people know it too.

◆ **Biography**. Do you have a special interest in and knowledge of some interesting person, either living or dead?

◆ **Business and management**. Do you have experience of some area of business that would interest others in the field?

◆ **Computer handbooks**. Can you unravel the complexities of computer and software usage so that the novice can understand them?

◆ **History**. Can you make people and events from the past come alive? There's a big demand for history books for both adults and children.

◆ **Mind/body/spirit**. A real growth area nowadays, with a burgeoning interest in alternative healing and the search for mystical knowledge.

- **Personal finance**. Do you have knowledge and experience that could help others order or untangle their financial affairs?

- **'How-to' books**. Do you have skills, experience and/or knowledge that other people would find helpful? There's a constant demand for books to show people how to improve their lives, cope with problems, develop hobbies and so on.

Recommended reading
Rachael Stock, *The Insider's Guide to Getting Your Book Published*.
Chriss McCallum, *Writing How-To Articles and Books*.

Now you should know:

- How to assess your idea.
- How to prepare and present a proposal.
- What a huge range of non-fiction books you can explore.

11

Writing for Children and Teenagers

Do you have a fund of ideas for stories, articles, games, puzzles, jokes and picture-stories? Could you write a 'young adult' novel, dealing with some of the serious issues that concern young people today? There's plenty of demand for all of these.

In this chapter:

♦ writing for children
♦ writing for teenagers and young adults
♦ crafting picture-stories
♦ writing non-fiction for children and teenagers.

WRITING FOR CHILDREN

Forget any idea you might have that writing for children is easier than writing for adults. It isn't. It's different, but it certainly isn't easier. Many a successful writer of adult material has failed in attempts to write for the children's market.

RED LIGHT
It's a big mistake to regard writing for children as a soft option.

There's no room for amateur attitudes here. Publishers receive shoals of stories with enthusiastic letters telling them 'My children (or grandchildren) loved this when I read it to them – I'm sure others will, too.'

Many of these stories arrive complete with unbelievably bad illustrations ('My friend has kindly done the pictures for you. She has always been good at drawing'). Unless your collaborator's work is up to professional standard, this will kill your submission stone dead. Publishers usually commission illustrations from a regular 'stable' of artists whose work they already know.

DID YOU KNOW?
Publishers send scouts round art colleges looking for talented illustrators.

Writing for children needs particular skills far beyond entertaining your own or your neighbour's children. You need to combine your adult language skills with the ability to get inside the mind of the child you're writing for.

And the younger the age group, the harder it is to cater for. The more simple and spare the writing, the more skill is needed to get it just right. When you read books and articles on the subject by successful children's writers, you'll see what a complex discipline it is.

Read the recommended books, look at the children's books currently in the shops, then decide if you could *really* produce the kind of material publishers want.

Some teachers believe that publishers don't really know what children like to read. They could be right, but to get your children's book accepted by a publisher you have to deliver what that publisher wants.

It's vital to study current markets. Many writers, especially older ones, tend to submit the kind of stories that were popular when their children (or even they themselves) were young. Their subject matter, language and treatment are out of touch with today's market.

— WISE WORDS —

Spend time in the children's section of the library and look at *recently published* books, both fiction and non-fiction. Study the various age ranges – note how the vocabulary becomes more challenging as the target age rises. Note the subject matter and treatment.

Don't send work to any publisher without first making a detailed study of their products in the age range and type of book you want to write. Every publishing house strives for a distinct personality and style. Buy some of their books, get out your coloured pens and analyse them down to the last comma. A vague notion of what the publisher wants will not be good enough.

Picture stories, puzzles, jokes, comic-strips

Look at the shelves of children's periodicals in the newsagents. Buy an armful and study the variety of material there. Most of what you see is freelance-contributed. Decide which ones you like best, then analyse them as you would any other magazine market, getting guidelines if you can.

There's a pretty fast turnover in new titles – not many achieve the long-term popularity of the old favourites, but it can pay to get in early when a new one appears.

There's a hungry market for puzzles of all kinds. You can usually find names and addresses inside the puzzle magazines themselves. Children love jokes and comic-strips are popular, too. Could you invent a character children would love – think Snoopy, Postman Pat, Bob the Builder!

WRITING FOR TEENAGERS AND YOUNG ADULTS

This is a constantly expanding market, with publisher after publisher launching new imprints to cater for teenagers and the slightly older 'young adult' market. There are great opportunities here for writers who can produce what these markets want. You must be able to write with understanding but without condescension, condemnation or preaching. You need to like young people. If today's teenagers horrify, disgust or alarm you, if you regard them as alien beings, it's probably best not to try.

— WISE WORDS —

Don't try to write for children if you don't feel comfortable being around them.

Subject matter

Today's markets embrace many topics that would have been considered inappropriate for young readers not so long ago. Most young people today, however, can identify with problems like divorce, single parenthood, homelessness, living rough, the 'generation gap', personal relationships, unemployment, shyness and so on. Stories about the problems of everyday living as well as traumatic situations can help young adults to understand and come to terms with the darker aspects of life.

The markets welcome writers who can treat such topics with understanding and sensitivity. Read a few books in these ranges to see if they interest you.

CRAFTING PICTURE-STORIES

Picture-stories are stories told in picture form, either drawn or using photographs. The illustrations can incorporate text as dialogue in 'balloons' and sometimes as captions in or below the pictures.

D. C. Thomson & Co. Ltd are prolific publishers of picture-story magazines for boys and girls of all ages from pre-school to teenagers. They will send you, on request, a comprehensive pack of information about writing story scripts, and will encourage and advise you if you show promise in writing the right kind of material for them. (Enclose a stamped A4 envelope.) Send for the guidelines and study the publications before you submit any material. Every magazine has its own characteristics, and you'll need to show an awareness of the specific requirements of any you choose to write for. Stories are not interchangeable among the magazines.

You won't have to supply the illustrations – they are done by commissioned artists – but you must present your script in such a way that the artist has a clear idea of what you want your readers to see in each picture.

The sample script (Figure 16) shows how this is done. It's a page from one of D. C. Thomson's girls' papers. You'll see that the speeches have to be very concise. There's no room in the pictures for long explanatory dialogue. The text and illustrations work together to move the story along. And don't lose sight of the fact that what you're writing is a story, not just a series of scenes.

— WISE WORDS —

Don't offer stories that are patronising or 'preachy'.

WRITING NON-FICTION FOR CHILDREN

Non-fiction offers a range of opportunities. Look at the success enjoyed by the 'Horrible Histories' series, for example, and activity titles like *The Dangerous Book for Boys*.

You need to be aware, though, that there are two distinct strands to children's non-fiction:

1. **Trade non-fiction** – the books and magazines that appeal mainly to the general market, the ones you buy from bookshops and newsagents. These range from the 'A is for Apple' books for tinies to teenage self-help books. Many trade publishers will consider *ideas* for books, but few will look at unsolicited manuscripts.

2. **Educational non-fiction** – mainly produced for schools and colleges. These range from language workbooks to history books and science textbooks, and are usually commissioned to fit in with the school curriculum. Your best (possibly only) chance of breaking in here is through personal contacts and institutions like colleges and universities.

Recommended reading
Children's Writers' & Artists' Yearbook.
Pamela Cleaver, *Writing a Children's Book.*
Allan Frewin Jones and Lesley Pottinger, *Teach Yourself Writing for Children.*

1 – Large heading picture. Leave space for title and the following introductory paragraph –

When Gary and Lesley Stark were orphaned in a road accident, they went to live at Springbank Children's Home.
   Gary and Lesley hoped to find a foster family where they could remain together, but had been disappointed so far. One day, Mrs Martin, the house mother, had news of a young couple who wanted to foster the twins –

Picture shows Mrs Martin talking to the twins in her sitting-room.
   Mrs Martin – *Mr and Mrs Hardy seem a really nice young couple. They love children, but they haven't any of their own, so they'd like you to spend a weekend with them.*
   Lesley – *That sounds terrific, Mrs Martin, but Gary and I won't build up our hopes too high. We've had a few disappointments already.*

2 – Caption – *But at first, the Hardys did seem to be the perfect foster-parents –*
Picture shows Mr and Mrs Hardy, a bright looking couple in their 30s, smiling as they lead the children from their car up the path to a small, neat terrace house with pretty front garden.
   Mr Hardy – *We've been looking forward to this weekend, kids! I hope you like our little house. It's going to be a bit of a tight fit with four people in it, but WE don't mind if YOU don't.*
   Lesley – *It looks lovely, Mr Hardy, and we LIKE small houses – they're cosy!*

3 – Caption – *Mrs Hardy showed Lesley where she was going to sleep –*
Picture shows Lesley looking puzzled as she looks around the small room with nursery furniture in it. The room has clearly been meant for a baby.
   Lesley – *Mrs Martin didn't tell me that you had a baby, Mrs Hardy. This room is a nursery, isn't it?*
   Mrs Hardy – *Yes, it is, Lesley. We did have a little baby of our own years ago, but she died, soon after she was born. We haven't had the heart to change the room since.*

4 – Picture shows close-up of Lesley looking thoughtful.
   Lesley – *Poor Mrs Hardy. It must have been terrible for her, to lose her baby like that. Let's hope Gary and I will be able to help her forget her sadness.*

5 – Caption – *At tea time –*
Picture shows Mrs Hardy serving twins boiled eggs, toast strips and glasses of milk. She and her husband have meat and salad and teapot set in front of them. Lesley is sitting next to Gary, glowering at him.
   Mrs Hardy – *Here we are, kiddies – nice eggies with toast soldiers, and lovely milk. If you're good, there will be stewed apple for afterwards.*
   Gary – *What! B-but ... oww!*

6 – Picture shows Lesley smiling sweetly at her cross brother.
   Gary – *You kicked me, Les. Watch where you're putting your feet.*
   Lesley – *Sorry, Gary.*
(Thinks – *I had to stop him complaining about the baby food Mrs Hardy has given us.*

Figure 16. A sample picture-story script.

Now you should know:

- What it takes to write for children.
- What it takes to write for teenagers and young adults.
- How to craft a picture-story.
- The opportunities open in non-fiction for children.

12

Writing Poetry, Song Lyrics and Greeting Cards

Some writers have a natural talent for expressing their thoughts and feelings in a few well-crafted lines. Others have to work on developing the necessary skills. Whether you are a natural or not, if you can produce inspiring work you can find outlets where it will be welcomed.

In this chapter:

- getting your poetry published
- how to set out a poem
- poetry 'on the air'
- where to get information about song-writing
- breaking into greeting-card writing.

WRITING POETRY

Poetry – the Olympic Games of writing. There's no money in it, unless you're lucky enough to win a major competition, yet the battle for publication and recognition gets keener by the day. Every poetry magazine receives thousands of submissions every year. Few have space for more than 50 or 60 in each issue, but that doesn't deter hopeful contributors.

GETTING YOUR POETRY PUBLISHED

Read other people's poetry

Writing good poetry is not just a matter of setting words out in lines, like chopped-up prose. Editors despair at the lack of craftsmanship displayed by so many would-be poets. You need to know how to combine the various elements of poetry to achieve the precise effect you want. The only way to do this is to study poetry closely, analysing how its elements work – sound, rhyming patterns, rhythm and form, all have a part to play.

Research the market

Read what is being published *today*. Unless you're in touch with current poetry publishing, you can't know what editors are looking for. Too many poets are sadly out of touch. Some are still sending work of 'Prithee, I come my troth to plight' vintage to contemporary poetry magazines. It isn't that editors only want 'modern' or experimental poetry. Far from it. Good contemporary poetry takes many forms. But editors still receive hopelessly archaic verse sent by poets who seem to have read nothing written this side of the Boer War.

TIP FROM THE TOP

Award-winning poet and poetry tutor Alison Chisholm advises:

> Read poetry. Enjoy the classics but concentrate on contemporary writing. This demonstrates how poetry works, and ensures that you absorb the poetic 'voice'. Read twenty poems for every one you write.

> Write frequently, pouring life experiences, observations and imagination on to the page. You will not always achieve a poem, but the more you practise, the easier the process becomes, and the better your writing will be.

> Revise ruthlessly. Never let a word, phrase, line, sentence or stanza appear in a poem unless it is the perfect vehicle to communicate your message.

> So to sum up – read, write and revise.

Get to know the magazines you like and support them

Every poetry magazine has its own distinct flavour. When you find one whose poetry is in tune with your own tastes, concentrate on that magazine, at least to begin with. Don't even think about sending your poetry to a magazine you don't feel comfortable with, or in which you wouldn't be proud to be published.

— WISE WORDS —

Don't send anything to a magazine you haven't seen – you risk your poems appearing alongside others you might consider inferior or worse.

Subscribe to at least one magazine, more if you can afford it. It's in your own long-term interest to help keep the poetry scene alive. You need these magazines as much as they need you.

When you're ready to try for publication

Present your work as shown in the example in Figure 17 below: typed, single-spaced with the stanzas clearly divided, and only one poem, however short, to a page. Put your name and address on every sheet – on the back if you prefer.

Unborn Children

These ghosts haunt differently, they come before,
Slowly, like secrets, pointing empty sleeves
From the margins of life, and promise more
Than the pattern anticipation weaves;
Some day I'll hear their laughter and their cries,
Touch their small hands and kiss their sleeping eyes.

They sing their coming in a swelling life,
The pleasure of our bodies' creating,
A helpless immortality my wife
And I can only tremble for, waiting
Until we hear their laughter and their cries,
Touch their small hands and kiss their sleeping eyes.

They are my laughter at the frightened years
When pain was loneliness and solitude,
My freedom from my generation's tears,
A promise of a sure familiar mood
When I hear their laughter and their cries,
Touch their small hands and kiss their sleeping eyes.

Mike Pattinson

Figure 17. Example of how a poem should be set out.
(Published in *Acumen* magazine, and reproduced here with Mike Pattinson's permission.)

Never send *anything* (even an enquiry) without an SAE. And please *don't* ask for free copies 'to see if I like your magazine' or 'to study your requirements'. Most poetry magazines are Small Press publications, struggling along on tiny budgets. Few make even a marginal profit. You should not expect them (or any other market, for that matter) to subsidise your market study and your postage.

Saving money, time and aggravation

◆ Don't submit poems to major publishing houses. A few do publish poetry, but a beginner's work seldom meets their standards. Wait till you have a respectable number of poems in print before you think about putting a collection together.

> **— WISE WORDS —**
>
> It's totally pointless to send single poems to book publishers.

◆ Don't send poetry to magazines that never publish it. They won't make an exception for you, however good you are.

◆ Don't send a saga the length of *Beowulf* to a small magazine where it would fill a dozen issues.

◆ *Never* send the same poem to more than one magazine at a time. This is 'multiple submission' and will damage your reputation. You risk a double acceptance – not the triumph you might think. Both editors will be embarrassed, and you won't be forgiven. Poetry editors see a lot of poetry magazines, and even if they don't see your gaffe themselves, you can be sure some indignant poet will 'advise' them.

Poetry 'on the air'

My thanks to Peggy Poole, prize-winning poet and for many years Poetry Consultant to BBC Network Northwest, for the following advice:

Outlets

If your local BBC or independent radio stations have no poetry programme, ask for one and organise area support. Poetry in the twenty-first century has a much higher profile than it has had for many years. Studio managers should be persuaded of this and alerted to the chance of a successful programme that will involve local listeners.

Submissions

Submit as for a top-class magazine, with an SAE. Keep poems relatively short – a rough line limit of about 40. (This does not mean the total exclusion of any longer work, particularly of a possible dramatic poem for several voices. In such a case it would be advisable to write to the producer in advance explaining the content, and a decision will be made either to present an extra, one-off programme or to vary the style of the regular poetry programme for that one special occasion.)

Do not use four-letter words, even if they are an integral part of a poem; this will jeopardise the programme.

Keep off politics, and ensure seasonal work arrives with plenty of time in hand. Humour is welcomed provided it is genuinely poetic and does not belong in a comedy programme. It's best to avoid nostalgic or pseudo-religious poems – huge amounts of these are received, but hardly ever used. Religious poems belong to religious programmes, and one person's nostalgia, unless of real quality, becomes someone else's boredom.

A good poem should work as well on radio as in print, but it is important to remember that your audience is probably engaged in several other occupations while listening, so your poem needs to work instantly at one level while offering resonances of deeper meaning at the same time.

Study this market, too
Listen to as much broadcast poetry as you can. Details of poetry programmes are given every week in *Radio Times*, for both mainstream and local stations. Do listen, even if your work is not being broadcast that week – only by listening can you get the flavour of a programme.

Reading
Many poets want to read their own work, but studios at the average broadcasting station are usually too heavily booked for this to be possible. It will depend on the producer and the length and format of the programme.

Payment
Do not expect more than a token payment. Remember you are reaching a very wide audience.

Checklist for poetry submissions
1. Each poem is typed in the accepted form on a separate sheet of plain white A4 paper.

2. Your name and address appears on every sheet.

3. You've kept a note of where you're sending each poem, so that you don't risk a multiple submission.

4. You haven't sent more than six poems at any one time.

5. You've enclosed a stamped, self-addressed envelope big enough and bearing enough postage for the return of the whole batch.

6. Always remember to keep a copy of every poem submitted.

Finding information and advice
The *Writers' & Artists' Yearbook* and *The Writer's Handbook* include information on poetry publishing, organisations and competitions. The Poetry Library (see page 178) will supply lists of poetry magazines, bookshops and current competitions. And there is a thriving community of poetry magazines on the Internet – simply search for 'Poetry magazines'.

Recommended reading
Alison Chisholm, *The Craft of Writing Poetry.*
Peter Finch, *How to Publish Your Poetry.*

GETTING STARTED IN SONGWRITING
Do you dream of writing a 'standard', another *White Christmas* or *My Way*? Do you watch the Eurovision song contest and think you could write something better? Maybe you could. From folk to rap, from traditional to pop, there's always room for a good new song.

You can't write music?
You don't have to. What you need is a collaborator. You write the lyrics, your collaborator writes the music and you share any profits.

Look out for sharks
The 'shark' is the music business's equivalent of the vanity publisher. He asks

for payment to write music to your lyrics. Don't throw your money away – no successful song has yet been produced in this way.

So how do you get started?

You can join a professional organisation, even if you're a beginner. You'll have access to sound professional advice and guidance. If you need a collaborator, you'll be helped to find one who will work with you, on equal terms, with no money changing hands either way unless and until your song makes a profit.

The Guild of International Songwriters and Composers is open to both amateur and professional songwriters. Services to members include:

- Free advice and song assessment service.
- Advice on promoting songs to music publishers.
- Legal advisers.
- Publishing companies' names and addresses.
- Copyright of works.
- Information on who requires songs for publishing and recording.
- Collaboration service.
- Songwriters' register.
- Song contests.
- A free quarterly magazine.

The Guild's website has all the information you need. If you can't access the Internet, send a stamped self-addressed A4 envelope for a free copy of *Songwriting & Composing* magazine, which gives information on the music industry and music publishing. If you have any queries about the Guild, phone or fax the Chairman, Roderick G. Jones, at the address given in Associations Open to Unpublished Writers at the end of the book.

BREAKING INTO THE GREETING CARDS MARKET

Greeting cards are very big business. According to recent figures, American citizens send out over ten million 'conventional' greeting cards *every day of the year*. And 'conventional' cards are only one category in a multitude of card types.

There's a fast-growing market here in the UK, too. Specialist card shops are springing up in every town. They serve a growing need: to help people express feelings they can't find the words to write themselves.

> — **WISE WORDS** —
>
> A greeting card sends a 'me to you' message, helping the sender to convey sentiments he or she doesn't know how to express.

Take time to browse. Most of the words and ideas for the cards you see in the shops have been bought from freelance writers.

Study the cards closely. While at first glance many of the lines appear similar, every company has its own style.

Could you write the kind of copy they use? Many companies print their addresses on the back of their cards. Some companies are specific about the way they like to be approached with ideas, others don't mind so long as the ideas are laid out clearly. Look at their websites. You'll often find detailed requirements there, as well as examples of the kind of cards they publish. If you can't find the information you need on the website, write to them and ask if they issue guidelines for writers and if they have any preferences about presentation. Don't forget the SAE. If the company has no preferences, print one idea per sheet on A5 paper, putting your name, address, phone number and e-mail address *on every sheet*.

Half a dozen ideas are usually enough to start with. The company might not buy anything from your first batch, but if they like your work they'll add your name to their list of writers and send you regular details of current requirements and urgent 'wants'. Don't give up if you don't succeed right away. (Remember that the only failed writer is the one who stops trying.)

> **— WISE WORDS —**
>
> Keep accurate records of when and where you submit ideas. *Never* send the same idea to more than one company at the same time.

Humorous cards offer the best chance of breaking in. They're the best paid, too. Here's one of my ideas bought by Hanson White Accord, reproduced here with their permission. (Most companies buy all rights – very few pay royalties.)

> Mother's Day:
> Page 1: You're a Mum in a million. Thanks for putting up with all the naughty things I've done ...
> Page 3: Good job you don't know about the rest!
> Happy Mother's Day

This card, illustrated by a commissioned artist, won the 'Mother's Day Best Humorous/Cute Card' category in the Greetings Industry Spring Awards in the year it was published. It's a good example of a 'sendable' card that would appeal to a wide range of buyers. The judges said they 'could all relate to it'.

TIP

'Sendability' is the key to success.

Payment
Payment rates vary, but most companies pay from £25 upwards (some pay £100+) for each humorous idea bought. (Payment for other lines, like sentimental verse, is a lot less.)

Finding information
- The *Writers' & Artists' Yearbook* has a helpful section, giving advice on breaking into the market, plus a selection of company names and addresses.

- The Internet – key in 'greeting cards' and marvel!

Recommended reading
Molly Wigand, *How to Write & Sell Greeting Cards, Bumper Stickers, T-Shirts*

and Other Fun Stuff – a mouthful of a title, but a treasury of tips and examples from a former Hallmark staff writer.

Now you should know:

- How to get your poetry published.
- How to get started as a songwriter.
- How to break into the greeting card market.

13

Writing for Radio, Screen and Stage

Do you have ambitions to write for the performing arts? There's plenty of scope. Radio and television in particular have an insatiable appetite for material. To break in, however, you need writing and marketing techniques different from those required in conventional publishing.

In this chapter:

- starting with radio
- writing for television
- writing for film and video
- writing for the stage
- getting your play published.

STARTING WITH RADIO

You'll have a far greater chance of breaking into television if you've already established yourself in writing for radio. Radio is by far the best starting point for new writers, especially playwrights.

In television, all productions are subject to budget restraints. Radio allows far more freedom. Anything goes. In radio drama, you can:

- Cast as many characters as you like. Because the actors are not seen, they can play more than one part.

- Take the listener anywhere in the world with appropriate sound effects.

- Set your play against any kind of background in any kind of weather, in daylight or darkness.

— WISE WORDS —

Radio stimulates the listener's imagination. As the often-quoted 'little girl' said, 'The pictures are better.'

Listen to as much radio of all kinds as you can. Tape programmes you like and analyse them. In plays, for example, note:

◆ How many scenes?
◆ How long are the scenes?
◆ How many changes of scene?
◆ How many players per scene?
◆ How many players in total?
◆ What kind of dialogue?
◆ What sound effects?

Make a note of the names of producers whose work appeals to you and try sending your script to them.

Radio talks

If you are an expert on some topic, think about offering a series of talks. You might read these yourself if your voice and diction are good enough, or they might be read by an actor. Listen to talks currently on the air – could you write something that would fit these slots?

Finding markets

The BBC (British Broadcasting Corporation) is one of the biggest markets for freelance writers. Radios 3 and 4 broadcast around 500 plays a year between them, and with the coming of digital radio, new channels are opening up all the time. There are opportunities for comedy, drama, short stories, panel game ideas ... the scope is as wide as your imagination.

The best source of information by far is the BBC website (www.bbc.co.uk) where you can access 'The Writer's Room'. Here you'll find all the appropriate addresses and guidelines for script submissions, including the required script formats. If you're not on the Internet, beg or bribe a friend to download the information for you.

> **RED LIGHT**
> You need these guidelines. If your script is not set out professionally,
> it has absolutely **no** chance of being read.

If you're interested in writing comedy, you can subscribe (free) to the Entertainment Writers' e-mail newsletter and you can apply for tickets to attend programme recordings. The *Writers' & Artists' Yearbook* gives a lot of information and advice on writing for radio and television as well as for film and stage.

Independent radio
Both the *Writers' & Artists' Yearbook* and *The Writer's Handbook* carry addresses for UK independent radio stations. Listen to your local independent stations – what kind of material do they broadcast? Are there any programmes you might be able to write material for? Never let *any* opportunity pass you by, however small.

Recommended reading
Shaun MacLoughlin, *Writing for Radio*.

WRITING FOR FILM AND VIDEO
Most film and video companies will only look at material submitted through an agent. Once you have a track record in any kind of published medium, you could try approaching an agent who specifies an interest in this field.

> **TIP**
> You need to present some interesting works in progress, and preferably also a portfolio of published work. They won't be interested in a total beginner.

However, there are a few companies listed in the yearbooks who will consider ideas. Comb this section for these companies, then look at their websites. The more information you can gather about the company the better your chances of pitching the right kind of ideas.

WRITING FOR TELEVISION

Do you watch plays and soaps on TV and find yourself muttering 'That plot's full of holes' or 'Terrible dialogue – really clunky', and think you could do better? Why not give it a go? The competition is hot, though, so you need to think carefully about your strategy.

TIP FROM THE TOP
The minute you send out a TV script you are competing with seasoned professionals as well as dozens, if not hundreds, of newcomers like yourself. Don't let this frighten you. It's not easy to write a TV script but neither is it brain surgery. Most people who want to do it give up too easily or simply don't learn enough about it in the first place. (Steve Wetton, from *Writing TV Scripts – Successful Writing in 10 Weeks.*)

To get a foot in the door of television writing, prepare a 'calling-card' script, as Steve Wetton advises in his book. Find a strong idea and write a 30-minute script. Send your 'calling-card' script to the producer whose work you most admire, to start with. If he or she is not interested, keep on pitching till you find someone who is.

RED LIGHT
Don't write a script specifically for a series currently appearing on television using the same characters. Such a script is likely to be returned to you unread, as the production company will not want to risk being accused of 'lifting' your idea.

Recommended reading
Chris Curry, *Writing for Soaps.*
Julian Friedmann, *How to Make Money Scriptwriting.*
William Goldman, *Adventures in the Screen Trade* and *Which Lie Did I Tell?*

Robert McKee, *Story – Substance, Structure, Style, and the Principles of
    Screenwriting.*
William Smethurst, *How to Write for Television.*
Steve Wetton, *Writing TV Scripts – Successful Writing in 10 Weeks.*

WRITING FOR THE STAGE

Your best starting point is a local repertory theatre or amateur dramatic group.
If you have no track record at all, it's unrealistic to expect to see your name in
lights in London's West End with your first effort. Not impossible, but not
likely.

However, management companies send scouts to repertory productions all over
the country. They are always on the lookout for original and potentially
profitable plays, and yours might be spotted.

Be careful to send only a play-script that could realistically be produced in the
venue and by the company you have in mind. A small theatre would not be able
to handle, for example, a play requiring crowd scenes.

Unless you already know someone in the company, it's usually best to write to
the producer first (by name) and ask if he or she would like to see your script.
Give all the relevant details: type of play, how many sets, how many characters
and so on.

You need to set out your play-script in a professional-looking format, so that
the different parts and the stage directions are clear. See Figure 18.

— **WISE WORDS** —

Never send anyone your only copy.

Read up on contracts before you sign any agreement. The *Writers' & Artists'
Yearbook* explains contracts in detail.

ACT ONE SCENE 4

(Into Daniel's fantasy) The stage remains in total darkness for a few seconds. Then we hear a voice off. It is Daniel's own voice but distorted and amplified to sound God-like.

VOICE: In the beginning there was the stadium. But the stadium was empty and the ground without shape or form.

There is a roll of thunder and a flash of lightning lights up the stage for a second. We see a deserted football stadium.

Darkness was everywhere. Then the spirit of God moved in the wilderness and said: Let there be light.

Lights up. But they are floodlights as at a football stadium.

This was the first day and it was good. But God saw that the stadium was empty and the gates were poor so he didst command: upon these terraces let there come forth all creatures great and small.

Football fans enter. Bewildered at first. Newly born.

And he called these creatures *(pause)* fans.

Explosion of music. Cheering etc. It stops as suddenly as it began.

Then God blessed these creatures and said unto them:
Go forth and multiply.

FAN: He said what?

VOICE: You heard. Go forth and multiply.

FAN: Right lads. Let's get at it. *(They try)*

VOICE: And this was the second day and it was good.
(Pause). But not that good for he had not yet invented women. *(Groans from fans)*

FANS: *(Chant)* Why are we waiting? Why are we waiting?

Figure 18. Example of how to set out a playscript.
© Steve Wetton. Reproduced with permission. From Steve Wetton's play
King of the Blues, performed at the Derby Playhouse. Not yet published.

Playwrights groups

Ask your Regional Arts Office for details of playwrights' associations in your area. Most of these groups hold readings and can arrange for script criticism.

GETTING YOUR PLAY PUBLISHED

It's well worth trying to get your play published, especially if it has been considered good enough to be given live performance by a local company. You can send your script to Samuel French Ltd, who publish nothing else but plays. If French's publish it, they'll include it in their *Guide to Selecting Plays*, a substantial catalogue of plays intended for performance by amateur dramatic groups.

You don't need an agent to approach French's, but they prefer that the play should have been tried out in some kind of performance. Performance reveals flaws that might have been overlooked in the written work and which you could correct before submitting the piece for professional consideration. They make no assessment charge.

French's will send you, on request and free of charge, their mail order list of books and cassettes on all the media and performing arts: writing, acting, production, make-up and so on, from Shakespeare to pantomime. (It helps if you can specify your area of interest.) You can find all the information you need on their website, too.

Theatre production companies

You could try making contact with some of the professional production companies who actively seek new writers' work. You'll find an encouragingly long list of such companies in *The Writer's Handbook*. Select those who specifically invite new writing.

Now you should know:

+ It's wise to start with writing for radio before you try television.
+ Where to get information on outlets.
+ How to get started in playwriting.

$$\boxed{14}$$

Self-Financed Publishing

Publishers do sometimes let a bestseller slip through their net, but they don't get it wrong as often as frustrated writers would like to believe. Many books are rejected because they're not remotely up to publishable standards. Many others are turned down because there is no ready market for them.

A publisher accepts a book and finances its publication because *in his judgement* it will enhance his profits or his prestige – preferably both. If your offering is rejected by publisher after publisher, but you still believe it has merit (or maybe you relish the challenge of going it alone), you could publish it at your own expense – and your own risk.

Do take a very careful look, though, at what is involved. If you get carried away on a cloud of 'publication at any price' euphoria, you could be in for problems.

In this chapter:

- ◆ is self-publishing for you?
- ◆ beware the 'vanity' publisher
- ◆ what a reputable publisher does
- ◆ self-publishing options
- ◆ publishing your own book.

IS SELF-PUBLISHING FOR YOU?

Ask yourself these questions, and answer them with ruthless honesty:

1. Do you have enough capital to fund your venture? Using traditional publishing methods, it will cost upwards of £2,000 to typeset, print and bind

a few hundred copies of a very modest book. Print-on-demand methods, though they allow you to order small print runs, will still involve a financial commitment. You can't avoid necessary expenses like registering for the ISBN system, costing almost £100 for the minimum ten numbers they issue, and the legal requirement to send copies to the Legal Deposit Libraries, as well as the actual cost of printing and binding the books you order. Don't offset sales against this outlay – there might not be any.

2. Can you afford to lose this money if it all goes wrong? Be realistic – any such venture has an inbuilt risk factor.

3. Have you assessed the competition? What books on your subject are already on the market? Will yours be better? *How* will it be better?

4. Have you identified potential sales outlets? (Don't include family and friends – they'll expect freebies.) Is there *really* a market for your book? If your subject is specialised, do you know how to promote your book to potential buyers? Do you know where it would be cost-effective to advertise? Publishing a book is not difficult – selling it might be harder than you think.

5. Do you know how to prepare the copy yourself (or are you willing to learn)? Do you have proofreading or editing experience? Do you know your way around typefaces and page design? If not, you must add to your costs: typesetting, copyediting (checking for typing and spelling mistakes, grammar, punctuation, syntax, ambiguity of meaning, errors of fact and so on), page design, typeface and paper selection, cover design and proofreading.

6. Do you have the time and stamina to go out and sell your product? (Even if you can afford it, you are very unlikely to find any representative willing to tout a single title from an unknown author around the bookshops.)

7. Do you have the time and know-how to promote your book on the Internet?

If you've answered 'No' to any of these, perhaps you should think again.

RED LIGHT

Can you *really* afford to lose all the time and money you're investing in the venture? If not, *please* don't do it.

BEWARE THE 'VANITY' PUBLISHER

He isn't hard to recognise. 'Authors! Does your book deserve to be published? Write to us ...' he sings from the national press. 'Publisher seeks manuscripts, all subjects considered ...'

RED LIGHT

'Proper' publishers don't advertise like this.

What a tempting song it is, especially if you're smarting from yet another rejection. But ...

Reputable publishers do not advertise for manuscripts

Why should they? They're knee-deep already. They can pick and choose. And they choose very carefully because they're risking *their* money and *their* reputation on their choice.

The vanity publisher risks nothing. He gets his money up front *from you*, and he has no reputation in the business anyway.

However loud his protestations to the contrary, he'll give you *no* editorial assessment, advice or service. He'll print your work exactly as you supply it, faults and all. His contract will commit him to print and bind only a small proportion of the copies you pay for, with an arrangement to print more as orders come in.

What orders? There won't be any reviews. He is well known to the book trade. No reputable reviewer or publication will promote his products. No bookseller will stock them.

So where does that leave you? Out of pocket, disillusioned, disappointed and angry. Left to do the selling yourself. And you might not even have any books to sell.

WHAT A REGULAR PUBLISHER DOES FOR YOU
When a regular publisher accepts your book for publication, he will:

◆ Enter into a legal contract with you, detailing the terms under which he will publish your book and giving full details of all rights and royalties agreed.
◆ Possibly (but not invariably) pay you an advance against the royalties you'll eventually earn.
◆ Arrange all the editing, designing, printing and binding.
◆ Handle warehousing and stock control.
◆ Arrange publicity.
◆ Arrange distribution.
◆ Handle all the accounting work.
◆ *Bear the cost of all the above.*

He'll do all these things to the best of his ability because *his* money and *his* reputation are at stake.

You won't have all this experience, expertise, organisation and finance behind you. You'll be on your own, and you'll be taking *all* the risks.

Be cautious about poetry, too
If you value your reputation as a poet, steer well clear of paying to have your work published by someone else. Avoid, too, those anthology competitions that have spread like a rash in recent years. No matter how good *your* poems might be, you'll have no control over the other poems selected. Your reputation could be badly tarnished, perhaps irretrievably.

Don't fall for these seductive advertisements. The risks are far too great.

SELF-PUBLISHING OPTIONS

If you're still undeterred and want to go ahead on your own, learn as much as you can about self-publishing. Read books on the topic, look on the Internet. The more you know, the better your chances of success.

Booklets and poetry

Low-cost methods:

1. Do the whole thing yourself, with a computer and a photocopier and stapler.

2. Have your text typeset and printed by your local 'instant print' shop and collate the pages yourself.

3. There might be a community press in your area with printing equipment. Ask at the public library.

If you have a little money to spend:

For a moderate outlay, you can have your poems printed and made up as booklets or greeting cards. Get prices from your local printer or investigate some of the printing services advertised in writers' magazines.

RED LIGHT

Make sure you're buying a *printing* service, *not* a publishing service.

Services you could offer:

◆ Could you produce your poems yourself in calligraphic handwriting on parchment or heavy paper? Mounted in photo-frames, these make popular gifts and sell well at craft fairs. With a bit of imagination, you could have tea-towels or T-shirts printed with your poetry. Look in *Yellow Pages* for companies who provide these services.

◆ Could you provide a service writing poems to order, for people to keep themselves or give to friends on special occasions like birthdays and anniversaries? You could offer a choice of frames or card mounts, all readily available from art shops or mail-order companies. You'll find these services in craft magazines.

PUBLISHING YOUR OWN BOOK

In my long working life in publishing, I've seen some writers achieve great success and satisfaction in publishing their own books. I've also seen many failures and much heartache, so I have mixed feelings about such a potentially costly exercise.

Publishing your own book is not a venture to take on lightly, especially if your manuscript has been turned down by several publishers. As Rachael Stock writes in her excellent chapter on the subject in *The Insider's Guide to Getting Your Book Published*, 'A bad manuscript self-published becomes a bad book.'

If you are seriously considering self-publishing, please do nothing till you've read as widely as you can about what is involved, as I advised above. As a beginner, you could be making an expensive mistake by jumping in without doing a lot of research.

The Society of Authors publishes a *Quick Guide to Self-Publishing and Print-on-Demand*. They also publish a list of publishing service providers who have been recommended by their members. Such recommendations are always worth considering.

If you're sure you can afford the risk, then, go ahead. Advantages include:

◆ Your book gets published.
◆ Your book gets published quickly.
◆ Your book gets published exactly as you want it.
◆ You control the whole editorial process.

- ◆ You control all the advertising and marketing.
- ◆ You keep all the profits.

Publishing your book via the Internet

It's easy to publish your book through services available on the Internet. There are many companies who will, for a small fee – and sometimes no fee – store your book electronically so that it can be downloaded directly or printed, bound and delivered to people who order it through the company's website. Look, for example, at lulu.com. The company takes a proportion of the selling price as commission. The idea sounds wonderful, but it means that potential buyers have to search your book out from all the other titles competing for attention online.

The same caveats apply as do to the vanity press: your book will be published in exactly the state in which you upload it, without any editing.

You'll also have to spend a lot of time and effort promoting your book yourself, getting reviews posted on as many websites as you can find, getting publicity in your local papers and in appropriate publications.

Publishing via 'print on demand'

The great advantage of print on demand over conventional publishing is that you can order your book to be printed in any number you want, from one copy upwards. You need no longer risk having your garage or your spare room full of unsold stock.

However, the process requires you to present your book in the form of electronic files compatible with the print on demand company's software. Unless you are technically proficient in this area, you'll have to budget for professional help with this.

Also, if your book is an academic, technical or reference title, it's essential to provide an index. Unless you have the ability (and the patience) to do this yourself, you'll need to hire the services of a professional indexer, whom you can find through the Society of Indexers (see under Other Useful Addresses at the end of the book).

And even before you hold the first copy of your book in your hands, you need to be thinking 'marketing'. How are you going to promote and sell your book to both the book trade and to the public? You won't have a publisher's sales team behind you – you'll have to generate all your sales yourself. You can publish the most exciting book ever, but you can't sell a book to people who don't know it exists.

Fortunately, there's plenty of advice available, both in books and on the Internet. You'll find all the information you need on both writing and marketing your book clearly laid out in Anna Crosbie's excellent book *How to Publish Your Own Book*, from How To Books, the publishers of this book. I recommend you invest in a copy and read it carefully before you embark on your self-publishing adventure.

Anna takes you through the whole process in detail, balancing the risks and rewards, and giving some enlightening case studies to help you decide whether this venture is one you have the ability, energy and means to take on.

— WISE WORDS —

You'll more than double your chances of success if you read widely about the business of self-publishing before you risk your time and money.

Selling online

If you would like to explore the possibilities of marketing your book online, read Aaron Shepard's self-published book *Aiming at Amazon* (see aaronshep.com/publishing). This author is making a great success of selling his books exclusively through online bookshop amazon.com, and shares his experience in this interesting book.

Whatever method you decide to follow, remember that the more you know, the greater your chances of success.

Recommended reading

Anna Crosbie, *How to Publish Your Own Book*.

Morris Rosenthal, *Print on Demand Book Publishing* (see www.fonerbooks.com).

Aaron Shepard, *Aiming at Amazon*.

Society of Authors, *Quick Guide to Self-Publishing and Print on Demand*.

Now you should know:

- If self-publishing is a viable option for you.
- How to avoid getting caught in the 'vanity' publishing trap.
- How to publish your poetry by low-cost means.
- The advantages of print on demand technology.
- Where to find more information.

15

Writing for Competitions

Competitions give you the chance to write stories and poems with more unconventional themes and a wider scope in style than those you could place in mainstream markets.

They also help you develop self-discipline because they require you to write to specific word limits and to meet set deadlines.

Search out competitions that offer publication. Getting into print as a winner gives you more than a prize and an ego boost – it gives you a record of publication to add to your CV.

In this chapter:

- ◆ which competitions to enter and which to avoid
- ◆ what you could win
- ◆ what the judges look for
- ◆ how to maximise your chances
- ◆ where to find out more.

COMPETITIONS TO ENTER …

Top of the list are well-established competitions like, for example, the Bridport Prize for poetry and short stories, the Arvon Foundation biennial poetry awards, the National Short Story Prize (Booktrust) and the V. S. Pritchett Memorial Prize. These competitions carry tremendous prestige in the writing world.

Look also for short story competitions in newspapers and magazines. Several top women's magazines run these regularly. *The Lady*, for instance, runs an annual competition and publishes the runners-up as well as the winners.

Many Small Press publications run competitions, often relying on the entry fees for financial survival. The better ones are well produced and have a healthy circulation (see Chapter 8).

Don't let fear of competing with experienced writers put you off trying the big competitions. Check the rules on the entry forms – if the entries are kept anonymous throughout the judging process, your work will stand on an equal footing with every other entry, no matter how famous their writers might be.

DID YOU KNOW?

Big poetry competitions are more like lotteries than contests. Usually, entries are divided among a panel of adjudicators. Each judge compiles a shortlist, then all the judges read all the shortlisted entries *only*. If a judge eliminates your entry in the first round, no one else will see it.

Each judge then selects a 'short shortlist' and the winners are chosen from these survivors – sometimes with a good deal of heat. Philip Larkin once said in public that his fellow judges of a major poetry competition had awarded the top prize to a poem that didn't make sense.

... AND SOME YOU WOULD BE WISE TO AVOID

There are many competitions around that could be classed as 'vanity' publishing ventures. These 'contests' invite entries, usually poetry, to be considered for publication in an anthology – only there is no real selection process. There are no losers. Every entry is awarded 'semi-finalist' status and the writer is invited to order (expensive) copies of the anthology in which their work will be featured.

Here, as an example, is a 'poem' I submitted under a pseudonym to one of these competitions, as an experiment. This effort won extravagant praise and was classed as a 'semi-finalist' entry:

Blackbirds in Spring

Blackbirds are nesting in our eaves,
Feeding their babies with worms and leaves.
Till one fine morning
Without a minute's warning
They all got up and flew away to Africa.

Would you be happy to see *your* poem in the same volume – perhaps on the same page – as rubbish like that?

WHAT YOU COULD WIN

Publication is the most sought-after prize of all. Competitions that guarantee publication of the winning entries attract by far the heaviest postbags.

Most cash prizes fall somewhere between £25 and a few hundred pounds. They're worth trying, as long as the entry fee is not out of proportion. Even a small cash prize can help fund entries to future competitions.

There are some 'biggies', though, like the Arvon competition, which offers a first prize of £5,000, with at least another £5,000 in other prizes.

WHAT THE JUDGES LOOK FOR

In poetry competitions, an adjudicator looks for:

- Craftsmanship.
- Controlled tone and language appropriate to the particular poem.
- Imagination and individualism.
- Conveyance of genuine feeling to the reader.

In short story competitions, the judges expect the same basic qualities a fiction editor looks for:

- A story that grabs and holds the reader's interest.
- A story that stimulates the desire to know 'what happens next'.

◆ A story that is soundly structured.

◆ A story that is fluently written.

Note, *a story*. Essays, personal memoirs, stories in poetry form, opinion pieces and the like are *not* short stories. Yet such pieces arrive for every short story competition – and are invariably eliminated.

DID YOU KNOW?

Eight-five per cent of competition entries are eliminated in the first sift, many because they haven't complied with all the rules.

TIP FROM THE TOP

Here's some excellent advice from competitions judge Iain Pattison, co-author (with Alison Chisholm) of *Writing Competitions – The Way to Win*:

If you want to do well in competitions, remember five things:

1. Read the rules – and obey them!
2. Give yourself ample time to hone and polish your work. Don't knock it out in a panic a few days before the closing date.
3. Tell a simple, powerful, moving story and keep it economical and tight. Don't show off with florid, pretentious, self-consciously clever word play.
4. Never forget it's a story, not a character sketch or vignette – plot is vital.
5. Don't be dull and ordinary – be original. Dare to explore dark themes, emotions and taboos.

Look at your entry with cool detachment. Don't submit a story that will cause the judge to groan, 'Oh no! Not *that* one again!' Here are ten plots that need a very long rest – if *your* story resembles any of these, think again.

1. **The ghostly hitchhiker**. Sally picks up a hitch-hiker on a quiet country road. Passenger vanishes, Sally staggers to nearby inn where gnarled ancient recalls local man's grisly end at that very spot fifty years ago to the day.

2. **Blind date**. Bored/sad/neglected Sally inserts/answers 'lonely hearts' ad. Surprise, surprise, blind date is equally bored/sad/neglected husband/lover

Jeremy; they clasp hands and vow to rejuvenate their relationship. Variation: Jeremy and Sally on a naughty weekend. Double meanings abound, till the last paragraph reveals them to be husband and wife.

3. **The man in the back seat**. Sally's car is chased by a maniac driver. She slews into a ditch, runs, pursuer catches her and lo! – it's her neighbour Jeremy trying to warn her that he happened to be looking out of his window and saw an escaped convict hide in the back of her car.

4. **The prize-winning roses**. Jeremy's perfect roses win local flower show. Sally the jealous loser pokes around his potting shed and finds suitcase belonging to Jeremy's wife who is supposed to be visiting her sick sister. Grisly remains found under rose bushes. Variation: Jeremy's roses begin to weep blood.

5. **Who's a clever boy then?** After heroic adventures/mischievous pranks and many coy hints, the narrator is revealed as Ginger Tom from next door/ Betty the Black Widow Spider/Billy the Bluffing Budgie ...

6. **The lucky day**. Racing correspondent Jeremy picks up a discarded morning paper, turns to the back page, reads that day's winners. Amazingly, the paper bears the next day's date, Jeremy bets a bundle and wins a fortune, then gets wiped out driving home. A gust of wind catches the paper, and we see a big black headline: 'Racing tipster dies in fatal crash.'

7. **The mutual sacrifice** (*pace* de Maupassant). Jeremy sells his treasured pocket-watch to buy an antique comb for beloved Sally, while Sally sells her flowing tresses to buy a gold chain for Jeremy's watch.

8. **Dreamtime**. Sally has a wonderful/terrible/amazing experience, wakes up to find 'It was all a dream'. Variation: the cyclical dream, where the opening sequence is repeated at the end ... Sally is condemned to live the dream over and over ...

9. **The far side**. Jeremy paints himself into a 'no way out' corner – 'And then, dear reader, I died!'

10. **Genesis**. Two children survive the end of the world, grow up, have two sons, call them (you guessed?) Cain and Abel.

In playwriting competitions judging criteria vary enormously, and reflect the differences in the facilities and economics of the companies organising them. Each competition should indicate its requirements clearly in its literature. You'll be working at an advantage if you can familiarise yourself with the venue where the winning plays will be performed – you can then avoid obviously impossible special effects and staging.

HOW TO MAXIMISE YOUR CHANCES

The DOs

1. *Do* read the rules. That's obvious? You should see how many people don't bother. It's foolish to invite elimination – if you infringe *any* of the rules, you're out, and you'll have thrown away your entry fee.

2. *Do* write what is asked for. If the competition is for a short story, don't send in an article or a memoir or a true story or anything else that is not clearly a piece of short fiction.

3. *Do* respect the stated word or line limits. The judges *will* notice if you don't do this and will eliminate your entry. They are bound by the rules, too.

4. *Do* study your 'market'. If the prize includes publication, it makes sense to study the magazine or newspaper that will print the winners. Make sure your entry is appropriate. Explicit sex, violence or over-strong language would not be acceptable in a national women's or 'family' magazine, or in a newspaper.

5. *Do* keep a copy of your entry, whether you're meant to get your ms back or not – and most competitions don't return them.

6. *Do* stick to the standard ms layouts, unless the rules state otherwise.

7. *Do* remember that judges, like editors, are human (yes, truly), and could be put off by bad presentation. Don't send a manuscript with handwritten amendments, overtyped words or patches of correction fluid. Reprint or retype if necessary. First impressions count.

8. *Do* allow time to check for misspellings, shaky grammar and ambiguous syntax.

9. *Do* comply if you're asked to write under a pseudonym with your real name only on the entry form and not on the ms, otherwise you'll be disqualified.

10. *Do* comply if the rules ask you to suggest a market for your entry, and *do* check that the market you name accepts contributions. You might consider your entry suitable for *any* market, but you must comply with the rules.

11. *Do* get your entry in well on time. If it arrives late, it will be disqualified, and you'll have done all that work and spent the entry fee for nothing.

— WISE WORDS —

Study and comply totally with all the rules – you'll be throwing away your entry fee if you don't.

And the DON'Ts

1. *Don't* enter *any* competition that requires you to surrender your copyright, however tempting the prizes. You could be signing away long-term benefits. Your poem might become a favourite for anthologies or even school textbooks, your short story might be adapted for radio or TV – it might even become the basis for a series – and if you've given up your copyright you'll have no right to any share in profits from any of these.

2. *Don't* enter any competition without getting the full rules of entry and reading them carefully.

3. *Don't* pack your entry in fancy folders, decorated cover sheets, ribbon bows and the like. They're a nuisance to the organisers and will go straight into the bin. (I once received a cardboard document wallet containing a mass of tissue paper covering a plastic sleeve holding a single poem.) Judges are wary of fancy packaging – it often covers the poorest entries.

4. *Don't* forget to enclose your entry fee. Nobody will send you a reminder. Your entry will simply be disqualified.

5. *Don't* contact the organisers after you've sent in your entry, asking them to make alterations to your ms. Get it right before you mail it.

6. *Don't* be too devastated if you don't win. Try a bit harder next time.

Competitions checklist

1. Have you read and complied with all the rules?
2. Have you written what was asked for?
3. Have you understood and applied any special instructions?
4. Have you kept your entry within the stipulated lengths?
5. Is your entry suitable for publication if that's part of the prize?
6. Have you presented your entry in the standard ms layout, on one side of plain white paper?
7. Have you kept a copy?
8. Have you completed and enclosed the correct entry form, if one is required?
9. Have you enclosed the correct entry fee, made your cheque or postal order payable to the designated name, and *signed your cheque*?
10. Have you enclosed a suitable SAE if one was requested?

WHERE TO FIND OUT MORE

◆ *Writers' News* and *Writer's Forum* run competitions and carry news about other current and upcoming contests.

◆ For information about poetry competitions, contact the Poetry Library.

◆ The bi-monthly *Competitions Bulletin* lists current and upcoming competitions, and also lists some results.

Recommended reading

Iain Pattison and Alison Chisholm, *Writing Competitions – The Way to Win.*

Now you should know:

◆ Which competitions to enter and which to avoid.
◆ What the judges look for.
◆ How to give your entry a fighting chance.

Glossary

Here are simple definitions of commonly used terms, to help you understand the jargon of the publishing business. Familiarity with these terms will give you the confidence you need in dealing with editors, publishers and agents, and could give you a useful edge on the competition.

Advance. Money paid to an author in advance of publication of his book. Under the usual terms the publisher will retain the author's royalty until the advance is paid off, after which the author receives his agreed share of the profits.

Advance Information sheet (AI). Publicity document giving sales and marketing information, issued by a publisher before publication of a book.

Advertorial. Article about a company or product used as an advertisement; the words 'advertising feature' usually appear at the top of the page.

Agreement. See 'Contract'.

Angle. Treatment of a topic to serve a particular purpose and influence the reader's response.

Anthology. A collection of stories, poems and so on which may or may not have been published before.

Appendix (pl. appendices). Additional section following the main text of a book, giving supplementary information.

Article. A piece of factual writing dealing with a single subject (or possibly several related subjects).

Artwork. Illustrations, photographs, ornamental lettering, fancy headings, etc.

Assignment. Request to a freelance from an editor to produce material on a specific topic; wordage, angle, fee and possibly a kill fee are usually agreed in advance.

Author biography/bio. Information about an author, including previously published works, often included in an Advance Information sheet.

Author questionnaire. Form sent to an author requesting details about his life for publicity purposes, and asking for ideas on marketing his book.

Author's alterations/author's corrections. Changes to proofs made by an author additional to corrections of typos etc. Might be charged to the author if excessive.

Author's proofs. Proof copy sent to the author for reading and correction.

Autobiography. A person's life story, written by himself.

Back matter. Material printed after the main text of a book: appendices, reference material, index and so on.

Backlist. A publisher's earlier titles that continue to sell.

Biography. A person's life story as investigated and evaluated by someone else.

Blog. A web-log = an online diary.

Blurb. Promotional text on a book jacket or cover.

Bullet. A large dot preceding and adding emphasis to an item in a book or article.

Byline. A line before or after a piece, identifying the writer.

©. A symbol signifying that a work is protected by copyright.

Caption. Descriptive note above, below or beside an illustration or photograph.

Catchline. Identification line at the top of a page of typescript or of a proof, discarded when the work is printed.

'Category' fiction. Fiction written to fit a specific genre: mystery, romance, etc.

Clip. A piece of published work cut or photocopied from a publication. Also called a cutting.

Collaboration. Two or more people working together to produce a work, sometimes published under a single pseudonym. (For example, Nikki Gerrard and Sean French, who write mysteries together as 'Nikki French'.)

Column. 1. Vertical section of writing on a page. **2**. Regular section in a publication written by the same person on the same subject or a related series of subjects.

Commissioned article/commissioned book. Article or book written to the order of an editor or publisher who promises to buy the finished work on agreed terms.

Commissioning editor. Editor whose job is to commission authors to write books.

Consumer magazine. Publication covering general affairs, sports, hobbies, etc. rather than business, trade or professional matters.

Contents page. Page at the beginning of a book listing everything it contains.

Contract. An agreement between publisher and author specifying the responsibilities each party undertakes in the writing, production and marketing of a book, in terms of payment, assignation of rights, timetable of writing and publishing, etc.

Contributor's copy. Copy of an issue of a magazine in which the contributor's work appears. See also 'Voucher copy'.

Copy. Term used throughout publishing for matter which is to be typeset.

Copy date. Date by which a piece of work is to be delivered to the editor.

Copyediting. Preparation of a typescript for the printer by a specialist copyeditor employed by the publisher to check facts, spelling and punctuation, syntax, etc. and possibly to rewrite clumsily written or inaccurate text, and to apply house style.

Copyright. Exclusive right in his own work of an author or other designated party, as defined by law.

Copywriting. Writing material for advertisements, publicity, promotions, etc.

Course book. Book used by teachers and students in teaching a course.

Cover letter. Letter sent to an agent, editor or publisher along with a proposal or manuscript or other material, giving the writer's contact details and any other necessary information.

Critique. Critical examination and written assessment of a work.

Crop. To cut off part(s) of an illustration.

Current list. Publisher's list of titles currently available.

Deadline. Latest date or time by which a job must be finished.

Defamation. Damage in writing to someone's name or reputation. See also Libel.

Department. Ongoing section of a magazine.

Desktop. The computer screen, where icons for programs etc. are shown.

Draft. Preliminary version.

DTP (desktop publishing). Computer programs for designing pages (text and pictures) on screen instead of pasting up on paper.

Earned out. Term applied when a book has earned royalties equal to the advance paid to its author.

E-book (electronic book). Book stored on computer file and readable on screen rather than on paper.

Edition. One printing of a book. A second or subsequent edition will have alterations, sometimes substantial, compared with previous edition(s).

Editorial. **1**. Introductory column in a magazine or newspaper, usually written by the editor. **2**. Text other than advertising copy.

Editorial calendar. Plan of a publication's future content.

Editorial policy. The editor's concept of the kind of publication he wants to produce.

Electronic submission. Submission made by e-mail or on a computer disk.

E-mail. Electronic mail, sent via the Internet.

E-zine. A magazine created and read on-screen.

Fact. A reality as distinct from an idea or belief.

Faction. Writing which blurs the distinction between fact and fiction.

FAQ(s). Frequently asked question(s).

FBSR (First British Serial Rights). The right to publish an article or story for the first time and once only in the UK. (Not used with reference to books.)

Feature. Magazine or newspaper article that is not one of a series. Usually refers to a human interest piece as distinct from a news item.

Fiction. Writing that is not and does not pretend to be truth but is entirely drawn from the imagination.

Filler. Short material used to fill a column when the text doesn't fill it completely. Can be applied to any short piece.

Flashback. Past action presented dramatically rather than narrated.

Folio. **1**. A leaf, i.e. two pages of a book back-to-back on a single sheet of paper. **2**. A page number. **3**. A manuscript page.

Font (Also fount). A specific design of typeface.

Foreign rights. Rights for work published in other languages for sale abroad.

Format. Size, shape and general layout.

Freelance. Self-employed person who sells his or her services or written work to a publisher for an agreed fee, i.e. a writer/journalist selling work to various publications but not employed by any one publisher. (Derives from the mercenary knights and soldiers who wandered Europe after the Crusades, hiring out their services and their lances.)

Frontlist. A publisher's list of books new to the current season.

Genre. A literary species or specific category, for example Westerns, romances, thrillers, etc.

Ghosting/ghost-writing. Writing a book in conjunction with someone as if it had been written by the other person, often with no credit given to the writer.

Gift book. Book designed for the gift market. Often in a small format and written to fit a particular niche – for mothers, fathers, grandfathers, cat- and dog-lovers, golfers etc. – and displayed near tills and check-outs to tempt the impulse buyer.

Gsm (grams) per square metre. Refers to the weight of paper.

Guidelines/writers' guidelines. Detailed specification of a publication's editorial requirements, terms, etc.

Hack. Derogatory term for someone who writes primarily for money.

Hard copy. Copy printed out on paper.

Hardback. Book bound in boards rather than paper or card. Also called 'hardcover'.

HB. Abbreviation for 'hardback'.

Hook. Strong beginning designed to grab and hold the reader's attention.

House. Jargon for 'publishing company'.

House magazine. Magazine produced by a company for its employees.

House style. Consistent style in which a publisher's books or magazines are produced.

Human interest. Material about people, their achievements, problems, ambitions, social and economic circumstances, etc.

Imprint. **1**. The printer's name, with the place and time of printing, required by law in many countries to be shown on published material. **2**. The name of the publisher with the place and date of publication.

Indemnity. See 'Warranty'.

In-house. Work done or ideas generated by a publisher or publication's own staff.

Internet. Global collection of computer networks with a common addressing scheme.

Intro. (abbreviation of 'Introduction'). Opening paragraph of a feature or article, possibly printed in bigger and/or bolder type than the body of the piece.

IRC (International Reply Coupon). Voucher sold at post offices worldwide, equivalent to the minimum postal rate for a letter from the country from which the letter is to be sent.

ISBN (International Standard Book Number). Unique reference number allocated to every book published, to identify its area of origin, publisher and title.

ISP (Internet Service Provider). Intermediary between the Internet and the user.

ISSN (International Standard Series Number). Reference number given to periodical publications in a system similar to the ISBN.

Journalist. Person who writes for a journal, newspaper, periodical and the like.

Justified setting/justification. Spacing out of words so that each line of text is the same length, flush left and right.

Juvenile. Term commonly used for children's books.

Kill fee. Fee paid to a writer when, through no fault of theirs, a commissioned piece is not used.

Landscape. Page that is wider than it is deep. Opposite of 'portrait'.

Layout. Overall appearance of a script or a printed page.

Lead. Journalistic term referring to the opening of a news story or magazine article.

Lead time. Time between the copy date and the date of publication.

Leader. Principal piece in a newspaper or magazine, a main story or article.

Libel. A statement written, printed or broadcast in any medium, defaming an identifiable living person by holding them up to hatred, ridicule or contempt.

Line art. Line drawings, e.g. cartoons, diagrams, as distinct from photographs.

List. Books a publisher has in print.

Literary agent. Person who acts on behalf of authors in their dealings with publishers, placing their work and negotiating contracts.

Little magazine. Small circulation magazine.

Mainstream fiction. Fiction dealing with traditional or contemporary literary subjects, as distinct from category or genre fiction.

Manuscript/s (abbreviation ms/s). Typewritten or word-processed text.

Market study. Analytical study of possible points of sale.

Mass market paperbacks. Paperbacks cheaply printed in large quantities.

Masthead. List of people who work on a magazine, with their work titles.

Matter. Term applied to a manuscript or other copy to be printed.

Media. Information sources: newspapers, magazines, radio, television, Internet news services and so on. (Plural of medium, i.e. 'medium of communication'.)

Midlist. Books that sell reasonably well but don't make the bestseller lists.

Modem. Device connecting a computer to a telephone line.

Multiple submissions. The same material submitted to more than one editor at a time.

Net royalty. Royalty based on the actual amount of money the publisher receives after deductions for discounts and returns.

Nostalgia. Genre (usually sentimental) recalling events and/or products of the past.

Novel. A fictional prose story of any length but not usually less than 50,000 words.

Novella. A short novel.

'On spec'/On speculation. Term applied to material submitted to an editor on a speculative basis, i.e. not invited or commissioned. Also applied to work sent at an editor's invitation but without any commitment on the editor's part.

Option. Right granted by an author to a publisher entitling them to first refusal of that author's next book.

Out of print. No longer on the publisher's list, i.e. no longer available except possibly from libraries or second-hand book dealers.

Outline. Sketched-out structure showing what an article or book will contain, but with little detail.

Outright payment/outright sale. One-off payment where the publisher buys all rights from the author.

'Over the transom'. American slang for the arrival of unsolicited work.

PA. Personal assistant.

Packager. A company that takes the concept of a book to a publisher and then oversees the creation of the project by writers, designers, etc.; the resulting product is then released by the publisher.

Page rate. Fixed or agreed rate per published page, regardless of wordage.

Paperback. A book with covers made of paper or card.

Para. Shorthand for 'paragraph'.

Payment on acceptance. The writer's dream scenario, all too rare nowadays: the editor pays for your work as soon as he accepts it for publication.

PB. Abbreviation for 'paperback'.

Pen name. A name other than your own that you use on articles and books.

Photo-feature. Feature where the pictures are more important and prominent than the words.

Photo-story script. A story told as a sequence of photographs with captions.

Pic/pix. Jargon for 'picture/pictures'.

Picture agency. Organisation storing photographs and/or illustrations and leasing reproduction rights.

Picture fees. **1**. Fees paid for the right to reproduce photographs and/or illustrations in which the user does not hold the copyright. **2**. Fees paid by a publisher to a writer for the right to reproduce his photographs or illustrations.

Picture-story script. A story told as a sequence of artist-drawn pictures, with dialogue shown in balloons, and perhaps with supplementary captions.

Piece. Jargon for any short piece of writing.

Plagiarism. The use without permission, whether deliberate or accidental, of work in which the copyright is held by someone other than the user.

Plot. The storyline, the central thread of a story with which everything that happens is interwoven.

PLR (Public Lending Right). System of monetary reward for writers, based on the number of times their works are borrowed from public libraries.

Podcast. A broadcast made via the Internet.

Portrait. A page that is deeper than it is wide. Opposite of 'landscape'.

Prelims (preliminary pages). Opening pages of a book: title page, publishing history, contents and so on.

Print on demand. An electronic process for printing books to order.

Professional journal. Publication produced specifically for circulation in a particular profession, e.g. *The Lancet* (medicine).

Program. Universally accepted spelling of 'programme' when related to computing.

Proofs. An impression of typeset matter for checking and correction before printing.

Proposal. Summary of an idea for a book, usually put to the publisher as an initial query, then as a sales package including a synopsis of the whole work with a sample chapter or two.

Pseudonym. A pen name.

Public domain. Material that has either never been in copyright or is now out of copyright is referred to as being 'in the public domain'.

Publication date. Date when a book is delivered to retailers.

Publisher's reader. Person employed to evaluate a manuscript and to supply a summary and report, to help the publisher assess its potential as a published work.

Pull quote. Quotation extracted from an article and printed prominently on the page.

Q&A/Question and Answer. Interview or other piece in the form of a series of questions and answers.

Query. Enquiry, by letter or e-mail, from a writer to an editor asking if he or she would be interested in seeing a piece of the writer's work.

Reader profile. The perceived average reader of a publication, assessed in terms of age range, social status, spending power, educational level and leisure interests.

Readership. Collective term applied to the people who regularly read a particular publication.

Reading fee. A fee charged by an agent, magazine or publisher to read a submitted ms. Usually refundable in the event of acceptance and publication.

Recto page. The right-hand page of an open book.

Remainders. Unsold books offered by the publisher to specialist dealers for a small percentage of the cover price.

Reprint rights. Right to republish a book, either in its original form or in a different format or version after first publication.

Reserve. Funds held back from the author against the publisher's estimation of books that might be returned by booksellers.

Returns. Unsold books sent back to the publisher from bookshops and distributors, for credit.

Review copies. Free copies sent before publication to book reviewers and other potential sources of publicity.

Rights. Those parts of an author's copyright which he leases to a publisher as specified in a contract.

Round-up article. Article containing interviews with or comments from a number of people relating to a specific topic.

RoW = rest of the world. Anywhere outside a specified geographic area.

Royalty. Percentage of either the cover price or the net receipts of a book payable to the author under the terms of a contract after any advance has been recovered.

Royalty-free copies. Books sent out for review or given away for publicity purposes, complimentary copies given to the author under the terms of the contract, or books returned from bookshops or wholesalers.

Running headlines. The headings that run across the top of the pages.

SAE/stamped self-addressed envelope. Envelope addressed back to the sender, bearing adequate postage stamps or sent with adequate IRCs. (US: SASE = self-addressed stamped envelope.)

Scanning. Process by which high quality printed text and photographs are read by computer scanner and converted into usable data.

'Scissors-and-paste job'. Contemptuous term applied to work that consists of material 'lifted' from reference books, encyclopaedias, magazines and so on, rearranged and then passed off as an original piece of writing.

Screenplay. Film script that includes cinematic information, e.g. camera movements, as well as dialogue.

Search engine. Electronic 'catalogue' capable of storing and finding an infinite number of website addresses relevant to a user's request.

Self-publishing. A venture in which an author publishes his book at his own expense. See also 'Vanity publishing'.

Serial rights. Rights covering material sold to magazines and newspapers. (Does not necessarily mean that the material will be printed in instalments.)

Setting. The process of turning typewritten or word-processed material into type ready for printing.

Shout line. A prominent line of text on a magazine cover drawing attention to an item featured inside.

Sidebar. Short feature accompanying a news story or article, enlarging on some aspect of the piece. Usually boxed or set in a different typeface or otherwise distinguished from the main text.

Simultaneous submissions. The same material sent to more than one market at a time.

Slush pile. Derogatory term applied to the unsolicited mss that accumulate in an editorial office. (So called because most uninvited material is romantic fiction.)

Small press. A small business, often a one-person operation, producing publications ranging from duplicated pamphlets to bound books of variable quality.

Source list. A list of the people interviewed and reference works drawn on in compiling a work. (Used by fact checkers to verify information in an article.)

Spam. Uninvited and unwanted e-mail.

Spread. Matter or illustrative material set over two facing pages.

Stable. Group of writers whose work is regularly commissioned and published by a particular magazine although they are not on its staff.

Staff writer (US: staffer). Writer employed and salaried by a publisher as distinct from a freelance.

Standfirst. Introductory paragraph in bigger and/or bolder type leading into and possibly summarising the content of an article.

Stet. (Latin) An editorial instruction meaning 'let it stand'.

Story. Jargon for a feature or article. (Not to be confused with fiction stories.)

Storyline. A distinct plot line, the sequence of events keeping the action of a plot moving forward: 'And then ... and then ... and next ...'

Strap/strapline. Identification line at the top of a manuscript page. See also 'Catchline'.

Style. The way in which something is written, e.g. short or long sentences and paragraphs, simple or complex language, etc. See also 'House style'.

Submission. Manuscript that is sent to a publisher with a view to publication.

Subplot. A plot thread subsidiary to the main plot line.

Subsidiary rights. Term usually applied to rights other than UK book rights, e.g. film and TV rights, foreign language rights, serial rights, electronic rights and so on.

Subsidy publisher. Another term for 'vanity publisher'.

Syndication. The selling of the same piece several times over to non-competing publications, possibly in different countries.

Synopsis. A précis or condensed version of the theme and contents of a book, giving a clear outline and breakdown of the proposed text.

Taboos. Subjects, words, references not acceptable to certain publications.

Tearsheet. Page torn from a magazine. Often used as an example of a writer's work when seeking assignments.

Technical writing. The writing of company and product manuals, reports, engineering and computing manuals and the like.

Text. The body of typeset matter in a book, as distinct from headings, footnotes, illustrations, etc.

Textbook. Book created for and sold to the education market.

Theme. The subject of a story, the basic concept that links the narrative, for example a moral concept – 'crime doesn't pay', 'love conquers all', or a specific human quality like courage or self-sacrifice. Not to be confused with the plot.

Trade books. Books sold through traditional outlets to bookshops and book clubs.

Trade magazine. Publication produced for circulation among practitioners and companies in a particular trade or industry, e.g. *The Grocer*.

Translation rights. The right to publish a book in a language other than the original language in which it was published.

Transparency. Photograph on slide film rather than in negative or digital form.

Unagented. Term applied to an author or a submission not represented by an agent.

Unsolicited submission. Work sent to an editor or publisher without invitation.

URL (Uniform Resource Locator). Address identifying an Internet document's type and location.

Usual terms/usual rates. The usual rates of payment offered by a publication to freelance writers.

'Vanity' publishing. Term applied to the publication of work on behalf of an author who pays someone to publish the work for him.

Verso page. The left-hand page of an open book.

Viewpoint. The point of view from which a story or article is told, the selected position of the author.

Viewpoint character. The character from whose viewpoint a story is told.

Voucher copy. A single copy of one issue of a publication sent free to a writer whose work appears in that issue, as evidence (to vouch) that the work has been published.

Warranty. The promise from author to publisher that material supplied is original, does not infringe copyright, does not include anything potentially harmful and will not lay the publisher open to claims of libel or damage. (Also called an 'indemnity'.)

Web log. See 'Blog'.

Website. Internet location set up by individuals or companies to promote themselves, their works and their services.

Word-processing program. Program using computer logic to accept, store and retrieve material for editing and printing out on paper or storing on the computer's hard disk or on removable computer software (CDs, floppy disks, etc.).

Workshop. A group of people meeting to exchange opinions and constructive suggestions on current work, usually under the guidance of a writer/tutor.

World Wide Web (also referred to as www or 'the web'). Network of graphic and text document 'pages' linked together electronically on the Internet.

Writers' circle. A group of people meeting to read, discuss and possibly criticise each other's work. Differs from a workshop in that the work is usually done at home beforehand instead of during the meeting.

Writers' seminar. A meeting of writers, often with guest speakers, discussions, possibly workshops, where writers can make contact with each other.

Young adult. Term applied to books for the teenage market.

Recommended Reading

Adventures in the Screen Trade, William Goldman (Abacus, 1996).

Aiming at Amazon, Aaron Shepard (Shepard Publications, 2007).

Bestseller, Celia Brayfield (Fourth Estate, 1996).

Blog Wild!, Andy Wibbels (Nicholas Brealey, 2006).

Book Business – Publishing Past, Present and Future, Jason Epstein (W. W. Norton, pb edn 2002).

Chicken Soup for the Writer's Soul, eds Jack Canfield, Mark Victor Hansen and Bud Gardner (Health Communications, Florida, 2000).

Children's Writers' & Artists' Yearbook, A & C Black (annually).

Copywriter's Handbook, The, Robert W. Bly (Owl Books, 2005).

Cracking the Short Story Market, Iain Pattison (Writer's Bureau Books, 1999).

Craft of Writing Poetry, The, Alison Chisholm (Allison & Busby, 1992).

Craft of Writing Romance, The, Jean Saunders (Writer's Bookshop, 2000).

Creating Short Fiction, Damon Knight (St Martin's Griffin, New York, 3rd edn 1997).

Editor's Advice to Writers, An – The Forest for the Trees, Betsy Lerner (Macmillan, 2002).

Freelance Copywriting, Diana Wimbs (A & C Black, 1999).

Freelance Photographer's Market Handbook, The, (Bureau of Freelance Photographers, annually).

From Pitch to Publication, Carole Blake (Macmillan, 1999).

Handbook of Magazine Article Writing, ed. Michelle Ruberg (Writer's Digest Books, 2005).

How to Create Fictional Characters, Jean Saunders (Allison & Busby, 1992).

How to Make Money Scriptwriting, Julian Friedmann (Boxtree, 1995).

How to Plot Your Novel, Jean Saunders (Allison & Busby, 2000).

How to Publish Your Own Book, Anna Crosbie (How To Books, 2006).

How to Publish Your Poetry, Peter Finch (Allison & Busby, 1998).

How to Research Your Novel, Jean Saunders (Allison & Busby, 1993).

How to Write a Blockbuster 'and Make Millions', Sarah Harrison (Allison & Busby, 1995).

How to Write & Sell a Book Proposal, Stella Whitelaw (Writer's Bookshop, 2000).

How to Write & Sell a Synopsis, Stella Whitelaw (Allison & Busby, 1993).

How to Write & Sell Greeting Cards, Bumper Stickers, T-Shirts and Other Fun Stuff, Molly Wigand (Writer's Digest Books, 1992).

How to Write Five Minute Features, Alison Chisholm (Allison & Busby, 1995).

How to Write for Magazines ... in One Weekend, Diana Cambridge (Canal Street Publishing, 2006).

How to Write for Television, William Smethurst (5th edn 2006, How To Books).

How to Write Realistic Dialogue, Jean Saunders (Writer's Bookshop, 2006).

How to Write Short Short Stories, Stella Whitelaw (Allison & Busby, 1996).

Insider's Guide to Getting Your Book Published, The, Rachael Stock (White Ladder Press, 2006).

Lessons from a Lifetime of Writing – A Novelist Looks at his Craft, David Morrell (Writer's Digest Books, 2002).

Light's List, ed. John Light (Bluechrome, annually).

New Oxford Dictionary for Writers and Editors, ed. R. M. Ritter (Oxford University Press, 2005).

Novel Writing – 16 Steps to Success, Evan Marshall (A & C Black, 2000).

Podcasting – The Ultimate Starter Kit, Steve Shipside (Infinite Ideas, 2005).

Print on Demand Book Publishing, Morris Rosenthal (Foner Books, 2004).

Professional Etiquette for Writers, William Brohaugh (Writer's Digest Books, 1986).

Schaum's Quick Guide to Writing Short Stories, Margaret Lucke (McGraw Hill, 1999).

Snoopy's Guide to the Writing Life, eds Barnaby Conrad and Monte Schulz (Writer's Digest Books, 2002).

Story – Substance, Structure, Style, and the Principles of Screenwriting, Robert McKee (Methuen, 1999).

Successful Non-Fiction Writing, Nicholas Corder (Crowood Press, 2006).

Teach Yourself Copywriting, J. Jonathan Gabay (Teach Yourself, 2003).

Teach Yourself Writing for Children – and Getting Published, Allan Frewin Jones and Lesley Pollinger (Hodder & Stoughton, 2002).

Touch Typing in Ten Hours, Ann Dobson (How To Books, 2nd revised edn 2007).

Understanding Publishers' Contracts, Michael Legat (Hale, 2002).

Web Design in Easy Steps, Richard Quick (In Easy Steps), (Computer Step, 4th edn 2007).

Which Lie Did I Tell?, William Goldman (Bloomsbury, 2001).

Writer's Guide to Copyright and Law, The, Helen Shay (How To Books, 3rd edn 2005).

Writer's Handbook, The, ed. Barry Turner (Macmillan, annually).

Writer's Market (Writer's Digest Books, annually).

Writers' & Artists' Yearbook, The, (A & C Black, annually).

Writing a Children's Book, Pamela Cleaver (How To Books, 2nd edn 2002).

Writing Competitions – The Way to Win, Iain Pattison and Alison Chisholm (Writers Bureau Books, 2001).

Writing Crime Fiction, Janet Laurence (Studymates, 2007).

Writing for Magazines, Adele Ramet (How To Books, 4th edn 2007).

Writing for Radio, Shaun MacLoughlin (How To Books, 2nd edn 2001).

Writing for Soaps, Chris Curry (A & C Black, 2002).

Writing Historical Fiction, Marina Oliver (Studymates, 2006).

Writing How-to Articles and Books, Chriss McCallum (Studymates, 2008).

Writing TV Scripts – Successful Writing in 10 Weeks, Steve Wetton (Studymates, 2006).

OTHER PUBLICATIONS MENTIONED IN THE TEXT

Book & Magazine Collector (monthly), Room 101, 140 Wales Farm Road, London W3 6UG. E-mail: bmceditor@metropolis.co.uk.

The Bookseller (weekly), VNU Entertainment Media Ltd, 5th Floor, Endeavour House, 189 Shaftesbury Avenue, London WC2H 8TJ. Tel: 020 7420 6006. Website: www.thebookseller.com.

Competitions Bulletin (bi-monthly), Carole Baldock, (ed.), 17 Greenhow Avenue, West Kirby, Wirral CH48 5EL. E-mail: carolebaldock@hotmail.com.

Directory of Writers' Circles, Courses and Workshops (twice a year), edited and published by Diana Hayden, 39 Lincoln Way, Harlington, Bedfordshire LU5 6NG. E-mail: diana@writers circles.com. Website: www.writers-circles.com.

Link, The National Association of Writers' Groups, The Arts Centre, Biddick Lane, Washington, Tyne & Wear NE38 2AB. Tel: 01262 609228. E-mail: nawg@tesco.net. Website: www.nawg.co.uk.

The New Writer (bi-monthly), Suzanne Ruthven (ed.), PO Box 60, Cranbrook, Kent TN17 2ZR. Tel: 01580 212626. E-mail: admin@thenewwriter.com.

Press Gazette (weekly), Wilmington Media Ltd, 6–14 Underwood Street, London N1 7JQ. Tel: 020 7324 2385. E-mail: pged@pressgazette.co.uk. Website: www.pressgazette.co.uk.

Publishing News, 7 John Street, London WC1N 2ES. Tel: 0870 870 2345. Website: www.publishingnews.co.uk.

Quick Guides – See www.societyofauthors.org.uk/.

Willing's Press Guide (annually), Chess House, 34 Germain Street, Chesham, Bucks, HP5 1SJ. Tel: 0870 7360011. E-mail: willings@romeike.com. Website: www.willingspress.com.

Writer, The (monthly), Kalmbach Publishing Co., 21027 Crossroads Circle, PO Box 1612, Waukesha, WI 53187, USA. Tel: 262-796-8776. E-mail: queries@writermag.com. Website: www.writermag.com.

Writer's Digest (bi-monthly), 4700 East Galbraith Road, Cincinnati, OH 45236, USA. Tel: 513-531-2690. E-mail: writersdig@fwpubs.com. Website: www.writersdigest.com.

Writers' Forum (monthly), editor Carl Styants, Select Publisher Services Ltd, PO Box 6337, Bournemouth BH1 9EH. Tel: 01202 586848.

Writers' News (monthly), editor Jonathan Telfer, Warners Group Publications plc, 5th Floor, 31–32 Park Row, Leeds LS1 SJD. Tel: 0113 200 2929. Website: www.writersnews.co.uk.

Writing Magazine (monthly), Hilary Bowman (ed.). Address and telephone as for *Writers' News*. E-mail: hgbowman@writersnews.co.uk. Website: www.writingmagazine.co.uk.

Associations Open to Unpublished Writers

Association of Christian Writers, Mrs J. L. Kyriacou, All Saints Vicarage, 43 All Saints Close, Edmonton, London N9 9AT. Tel: 020 8884 4348. E-mail: admin@christianwriters.org.uk.

British Fantasy Society, 201 Reddish Road, Stockport SK5 7HR. Tel: 0161 476 5368 (after 6 pm). E-mail: faliol@yahoo.com. Website: britishfantasysociety.org.uk.

British Science Fiction Association (President Arthur C. Clarke), Estelle Roberts, 97 Sharp Street, Newland Avenue, Hull HU5 2AE. E-mail: bsfa@enterprise.net.

Guild of International Songwriters and Composers, Sovereign House, 12 Trewartha Road, Praa Sands, Penzance, Cornwall TR20 9ST. Tel: 01736 762826. E-mail: songmag@aol.com. Website: www.songwriters-guild.co.uk.

Historical Novel Society, Richard Lee (Secretary), Marine Cottage, The Strand, Starcross, Devon EX6 8NY. Tel: 01626 891962. E-mail: histnovel@aol.com. Website: www.historicalnovelsociety.com.

National Association of Writers' Groups, The Arts Centre, Biddick Lane, Washington, Tyne & Wear NE38 2AB. Tel: 01262 609228. E-mail: nawg@tesco.net. Website: www.nawg.co.uk.

Player-Playwrights, Secretary Peter Thompson, 9 Hillfield Park, London N10 3QT. Tel: 020 8883 0371. E-mail: p-p@dila.pipex.com. Website: www.player-playwrights.co.uk.

Romantic Novelists' Association, Secretary Eileen Ramsay, Bonnyton House, Arbirlot, Angus DD11 2PY. Tel: 01241 874131. Website: www.rna-uk.org.

Society of Civil and Public Service Writers, Secretary Mrs J. M. Lewis, 17 The Green, Corby Glen, Grantham, Lincs NG33 4NP. E-mail: joan@lewis5643.fsnet.co.uk.

Note: The *Writers' & Artists' Yearbook* lists a wide range of writing-related societies, associations and clubs in various regions around the UK.

Other Useful Addresses

Arts Council of England, 14 Great Peter Street, London SW1P 3NQ. Tel: 0845 300 6200. Fax: 020 7973 6590. E-mail: enquiries@artscouncil.org.uk. Website: www.artscouncil.org.uk.

Arvon Foundation, 42A Buckingham Palace Road, London SW1W 0RE. www.arvonfoundation.org.

Association of Authors' Agents, 20 John Street, London WC1N 2DR. Tel: 020 7405 6774. Fax: 020 7831 2154. E-mail: aaa@johnsonandalcock.co.uk. Website: www.agentsassoc.co.uk.

Authors' Licensing & Collecting Society Ltd, The Writer's House, 13 Haydon Street, Holborn, London EC3N 1DB. Tel: 020 7264 5700. E-mail: alcs@alcs.co.uk. Website: www.alcs.co.uk.

BAFTA (British Academy of Film and Television Arts), 195 Piccadilly, London W1J 9LN. Tel: 020 7734 0022. Fax: 020 7292 5868. E-mail: reception@bafta.org. Website: www.bafta.org.

BBC (British Broadcasting Corporation), Broadcasting House, Portland Place, London W1A 1AA. Website: www.bbc.co.uk.

BBC Writers' Room, 1 Mortimer Street, London W1T 3JA. Website: www.bbc.co.uk/writersroom.

Booktrust (formerly the National Book League), Book House, 45 East Hill, London SW18 2QZ. Tel: 020 8516 2977. Fax: 020 8516 2998. E-mail: info@booktrust.org.uk. Website: www.booktrust.org.uk.

British Academy, 10 Carlton House Terrace, London SW1V 5AH. Tel: 020 7969 5200. Fax: 020 7969 5300. E-mail: secretary@britac.ac.uk. Website: www.britac.co.uk.

British Council, 10 Spring Gardens, London SW1A 2BN. Tel: 020 7930 8466. Fax: 020 7839 6347. Website: www.britishcouncil.org.

Flair for Words, 14 Leonard Hackett Court, St Winifred's Road, Meyrick Park, Bournemouth BH2 6PR. Website: www.flair4words.co.uk.

National Union of Journalists, Headland House, 308–312 Gray's Inn Road, London WC1X 8DP. Tel: 020 7278 7916. Fax: 020 7837 8143. E-mail: acorn.house@nuj.org.uk.

Poetry Library, Level 5, Royal Festival Hall, London SE1 8XX. Tel: 020 7921 0943. E-mail: poetrylibrary@rfh.org.uk. Website: www.poetrylibrary.org.uk.

Samuel French Ltd, 52 Fitzroy Street, London W1T 5JR. Tel: 020 7387 4373. Website: www.samuelfrench-london.co.uk.

Society for Editors and Proofreaders (SfEP), Riverbank House, 1 Putney Bridge Approach, London SW6 3JD. Tel: 020 7736 3278. E-mail: admin@sfep.org.uk. Website: www.sfep.org.uk.

Society of Authors, 84 Drayton Gardens, London SW10 9SB. Tel: 020 7373 6642. E-mail: info@societyofauthors.org. Website: www.societyofauthors.org.

Society of Indexers, Woodbourne Business Centre, 10 Jessell Street, Sheffield S9 3HY. Website: www.indexers.org.uk.

Society of Women Writers & Journalists (SWWJ), Membership Secretary Wendy Hughes, 27 Braycourt Avenue, Walton-on-Thames, Surrey KT12 2AZ. Tel: 01932 702874. E-mail: wendy@stickler.org. Website: www.swwj.co.uk.

Winchester Writers' Conference, University of Winchester, Winchester, Hants SO22 4NR. Tel: 01962 827238. E-mail: barbara.large@winchester.ac.uk. Website: www.writersconference.co.uk.

Writers' Guild of Great Britain, 15 Britannia Street, London WC1X 9JN. Tel: 020 7833 0777. Fax: 020 7833 4777. E-mail: admin@writersguild.org.uk. Website: www.writersguild.org.uk.

Writers' Holiday in Wales at Caerleon, contact D. L. Anne Hobbs, School Bungalow, Church Road, Pontnewydd, Cwmbran, South Wales NP44 1AT at any time with a stamped self-addressed envelope for details and a booking form. Tel: 01633 489438. Website: http://website.lineone.net/~writersholiday/.

Writers' Summer School at Swanwick, contact secretary Jean Sutton, 4 Home Farm Close, Sandown, Isle of Wight PO36 9QF, enclosing a stamped self-addressed envelope. Tel: 01983 406759. Website: www.wss.org.uk.

Index